A BAG OF

ON A TREASURE HUNT WITH GOD

Includes Personal Growth or Small Group Discussion Guide

PATTY WILLIAMS

A Bag of Blue
On a Treasure Hunt with God
Patty Williams

To contact the author: pwilliams5757@icloud.com

Published by

Mary Ethel

Mary Ethel Eckard
Frisco, Texas

Library of Congress Control Number: 2024909234
ISBN (Print): 979-8-9904576-6-9
ISBN (Ebook): 979-8-9904576-7-6

Cover Photos:

Patty is seen climbing to the summit of Croagh Patrick, a mountain with a height of 764m and an important site of pilgrimage in County Mayo, Ireland. The mountain has a pyramid-shaped peak and overlooks Clew Bay, rising above the village of Murrisk. It has long been seen as a holy mountain and is associated with Saint Patrick, who is said to have spent forty days fasting on the summit. Patty's great grandfather, Patrick Taugher, was from Ireland; which made the climb especially meaningful to her.

Front cover photo taken by Katie Keefe.
Back cover photo taken by Jim Zemanick.

CONTENTS

Dedication v

Foreword... ix

Introduction xiii

Chapter 1   Blue Flip-Flop................................. 1
Chapter 2   Blue Spoon 9
Chapter 3   Blue Lighter 17
Chapter 4   Blue Pen... 25
Chapter 5   Blue Broken Glass........................ 35
Chapter 6   Blue Earplugs................................ 43
Chapter 7   Blue Odds / Blue Mountain Lake .. 53
Chapter 8   Blue Dru / Blue Glove 59
Chapter 9   Blue Coat....................................... 69
Chapter 10 Blue Ends 79

A Blessing Before You Go................................ 87
Questions for Personal Growth or Small Group Discussion 89
About the Author..113
Notes 115

DEDICATION

Figure 1 My family, my treasure
Top left: John & Patty / Top right: Lindsey & Ryan / Bottom left:
Dominic, Sophie & Rachel / Bottom right: Karissa

I am so grateful for my family. John, you are a humble, loving man with profound wisdom and integrity. I am so blessed to be your bride. Lindsey, Ryan, Dominic, Sophie, Rachel and Karissa. I don't know why God found me worthy to have such amazing children, but He did. Thanks be to God, He did! I love you all.

Mom and Dad, the love you have given us over the years and sacrifices you've made for our great big Zemanick family, did not go unnoticed. You have given our family a strong foundation. You have been there for us in good times and bad. This story would have been pretty boring if it weren't for you two. Love you both.

To my siblings… Mary, Jim, Louise, John and Amy. While you are my brothers and sisters, you are my best friends. What a gift I have in you and your beautiful families too. I love you all and cherish the memories we share.

To my other besties in life. Mary Ethel Eckard, Amy O'Brien and Jade Cohen. I am so blessed to have such dear friends. Time and distance changes nothing; we always pick up right where we left off. Thank you for your wisdom and encouragement, my beloved friends.

Nancy Williams (Mom)… Jesus knocked at your heart's door and you opened it. You are a woman of great faith and courage; a trailblazer pointing the way of Truth for others to follow. You are precious to Him and to our family.

Luna, you are my little sunshine. Being your *Mimi* has given me so much joy. This book is especially for you and for ALL of my future grandchildren, great-grandchildren, and generations to come… Times are getting harder and being a person of faith more challenging. When hard days come, and they will come, know that you are not alone. You have a huge family here on earth and in heaven, praying for you and cheering you on. Press on. God is with you. Keep the faith. You are loved.

In memory of Stacy (Cortese) Williams
January 31, 1969 - July 25, 2006

Figure 2 Hugs from Mimi

Therefore, we do not lose heart. Even though our outward man is perishing, yet the inward man is being renewed day by day. For our light affliction, which is but a moment, is working for us a far more exceeding and eternal weight of glory, while we do not look at the things which are seen, but at the things which are not seen. For the things which are seen are temporary, but the things which are not seen are eternal.
2 Corinthians 4:16-18 (NLT)

FOREWORD

Your heart, soul, mind, and spirit are about to be lifted. Not by what I'm writing in the Foreword, but by the book you are holding in your hands and the stories contained within. Stories about the goodness of God recounted in such a way that you, too, will stand amazed at His wonders and workings. Prepare yourself to see how He pursues and interacts with His most prized possession – you! By the time you are finished with this book, you will understand my total admiration and spiritual infatuation with this amazing, restored, and inspirational woman of God. Not because of who she is, but because of who He is within her. She truly reflects the light of Jesus Christ. Allow me to introduce you to this author who God used to change my life.

In 1998, I wasn't looking for a friend. I had one, and I thought my life was at capacity. Little did I know that God was about to capture me with one of the greatest arrows in His quiver. One day, she came into the office, professionally dressed in a business suit, wearing high heels, hair flowing like a L'oreal shampoo commercial, and a big smile on her face. Clearly, she didn't get the memo that new employees need not bring up the dress code of a corporate office.

After being introduced, Patty was assigned the desk next to mine. When she turned to look at me, I smiled and, matter-of-factly, said, "If you ever dress like that again to come into this office, you are so fired." Not that I had the authority to hire or fire anyone. I was an executive secretary and so was she. Seeing through my words, we both laughed. It seems I did need another friend.

Soon after, Patty came into the office excited to tell me about something that happened on her way to work. I don't remember what the story was about, but I do remember the main character was God. I rolled my eyes. I hadn't met anyone, ever, who told stories about God that made Him so present, approachable, and involved in our everyday life. With every God-story that rolled off her tongue, I rolled my eyes.

Over time, as Patty's stories continued, my eyes came into focus as my heart hungered for more of God. I wanted what she had. She saw God in everything; in nature, in people, in everyday circumstances. Her storytelling awakened my desire to know Him as she did. I joined a Bible study she was leading. I accepted her invitation to a women's retreat. I attended prayer gatherings with her. I followed her everywhere because she was on the path that would lead me to Him. Soon I found myself in His presence, sitting at His feet, listening to His words, asking for a heart of obedience to follow Him, no matter the cost.

Then, God called me to start a website ministry. It was Patty who wrote the first blog. Through her life lessons, I discovered her ability to write and tell stories with vulnerability and authenticity. I observed her walk through many life situations, both uphill and downhill, and I learned what it meant to be a sold-out believer. Her life taught me that God is real, hearing Him is possible, and leaning into Him is the only way.

Patty and I have walked together for twenty-six years. We have hiked the highest peaks and crawled the lowest valleys, seeing God's miracles and majesty in the heights and depths. Within these pages, you, too, will experience just a tad of Patty, and you will want more. More of her stories, more understanding of how she sees God in everything -everyone -everywhere; but mostly, you will want more of

Him. Just as I did after meeting her. She's that kind of person. Her love for the Lord is contagious, her courage is admirable, and her heart calls to the reader, "Come and sit with my Jesus and your life will be forever changed."

Be prepared to be challenged, to have your spiritual eyes and ears opened to the everyday sights and sounds around you, and to ponder these God stories long after you have closed this book.

I love Patty Williams and you will too. Guaranteed.

Mary Ethel Eckard
Author, *The Making of a Dragonfly* and *Lessons of a Dragonfly*

INTRODUCTION

MARY'S DRAGONFLY
& A BAG OF BLUE

When you call on me, when you come and pray to me, I'll listen.
When you come looking for me, you'll find me.
Yes, when you get serious about finding me and
want it more than anything else,
I'll make sure you won't be disappointed.
Jeremiah 29:12-14 (MSG)

Before I tell you about my *Bag of Blue* and how this whole thing came to be, there's another story to share. It isn't my own. It belongs to my forever friend, Mary Ethel Eckard. Her story is uniquely hers and a great one at that. She has shared it many times and has given me express written consent to use it now. Just kidding… while I did ask for her permission to include her story in this book, she skipped the formalities and just said, "go for it!" She isn't the stuffy sort. She's the polar opposite of that. Come with me. I can't wait for you to meet her…

May 2001 – Plano, Texas. Mary was searching for something. The something she was looking for wasn't for herself; it was for her sons. Two little boys with a school project of collecting dead insects. They had quite an extensive list. Repeatedly they scoured their neighborhood, found insects lying on the ground (already dead of course), put them in their box and checked them off their list. Tyler and Patrick had been very successful on their own, yet after many insect hunting expeditions there was just one that continued to elude them – a dragonfly. What did they do? Just what most children do – enlist the help of a loving parent. "Mom, can you help us find a dragonfly?" Why, of course she would!

The boys went to school. Mary stepped out the front door. It was another sunny day in Texas. It wasn't long before Mary realized that finding a dead dragonfly was a tall order. She headed back home empty handed. Several daily walks produced the same results... she remained dragonfly-less. What's a mom to do? Just what any mom in her circumstance would do – enlist the help of a loving parent. But not just any parent, a super-hero kind of parent. The One who breathed life into her lungs, the One who created the universe, and the One who created the darned old dragonfly in the first place... none other than her loving father, God.

But would He be willing to help her? She thought about it. They hadn't talked in a while. It wasn't that He hadn't been willing to – it was her. She knew that. You see, there was an odd dance they did...

> He'd reach out.
> She'd take His hand.
> She'd draw close.
> Then back again.

Why did she periodically withdraw from Him anyway?! Deep down she had a sense that God still loved her. At least she wanted to believe He did. So – did He? Did He really love her? She needed to know. Everything in her cried out to know – REALLY, REALLY KNOW – that He loved her <u>uniquely</u>! That she mattered to Him.

Mary turned her face to the vast Texas sky, closed her eyes under the morning sun and began to pray...

> *Lord, if you love me, if you are real, if you truly have plans for my life, would you give me a dead dragonfly for this insect collection?*

So, what did her Father do? Love His precious child. God's love doesn't mean we always get what we ask for unless what we ask for is in line with His will. Yet on that particular day, it was clear that He willed for Mary to know His infinite love, so when she turned her eyes once again to the sidewalk, there at her feet was a dead dragonfly. God melted her heart.

Turns out that the "something" Mary was searching for was far more than a dragonfly. She was searching for the truth about God's love. That it was real. Really, really REAL! That morning her faith grew wings and was the beginning of one of the sweetest, most tender, trusting love relationships I have had the privilege of witnessing.

Today, more than 20 years later, Mary remains completely obedient to God because she has absolute faith in her Father who adores her and that He'd never lead her astray. So, when He says I need you to do this or move there, she says... "Okay, let's go!" And they (she and God) are on their way to accomplish something that will glorify Him. One of those things they've accomplished together is a beautiful book entitled, "The Making of a Dragonfly: Following Christ through the Winds of Change." You might want to add that to your reading list. You won't be able to put it down.

Thank you, Mary, for your story of God revealing Himself to you. It was on my heart the morning a *Bag of Blue* unfolded...

Figure 3 With my best friend, Mary Ethel Eckard

August 2015 – Port Crane, NY. I don't know what I was thinking, honestly. The year started out just fine, doing a little bit here, a little bit there, until one day I woke up completely exhausted and not feeling that I was doing any particular thing very well. My husband and kids had slipped in my list of priorities, which should have sounded an alarm to slow down – but I didn't. I was doing things that I thought God wanted me to do, but in the final analysis, I had to ask myself a hard question. Am I doing all the extra stuff for Him or for me? What are my true motives? Those were the things that were heavy on my heart as I started out for my morning walk with God.

Our home is in the country, which is a very good thing because I get to take my walks on roads that twist along a tree lined ravine, up and down hills, past barns and cow pastures... so beautiful. There aren't many vehicles driving by or other walkers. Just me and God. We have a lot of privacy, so I feel comfortable praying/talking aloud. My prayer this morning went something like this...

God, I'm so tired. I want to please you, but this isn't working. I'm completely exhausted. Help me, Lord. I want to do Your will, but I need clarity. I need your guidance in my life. When Mary asked You for a dragonfly – You gave it to her. So, if You love me too, would You give me something all of my own? I'm humbly asking for a sign that will give me some direction. I'm not going to look to the left or to the right, I'm going to look directly on the road I'm traveling along – that way I'll know it's from You. Father, I long to serve You and be present to my family, with a renewed Spirit so I trust You will work this out. Amen.

About a mile into the walk there was something directly in front of me on the road. A blue object. A few steps closer and I could see that it was a blue flip-flop. *God, is this from you? That's odd.* I picked it up thinking that if it was from Him, it wasn't what I was expecting. And, if it was a sign, what could the flip-flop mean. Strange as it was, I decided to carry it with me.

Another quarter mile, at my feet I saw a children's spoon with a bright blue handle. I picked that up as well. Another sign? *Weird.* I continued on with the flip-flop in one hand and the spoon in the other.

Just a few yards past the spoon there was a blue lighter. I rolled my finger over the spark wheel and a flame appeared. Now I had a blue flip-flop, a blue spoon, a blue lighter... all blue things, and the strange part of it was I didn't pass other miscellaneous items along the way. I wasn't hunting and picking just blue things – they were the ONLY things. I scratched my head and moved along.

At the 2 ½ mile point in my walk, yet another blue object. A blue pen this time. I set the flip-flop, spoon and lighter down on the ground and lifted the pen with my right hand and attempted to scribble on my left palm. *Hey... it still writes. Cool! Is this another clue God? This is fun!* I gathered up all of my belongings, by now wishing for a bag. I didn't ask for a bag, and He didn't seem to be offering one either because I didn't come across a blue bag.

At three miles, there were several small pieces of cobalt blue broken glass. You guessed it. I picked them up too – ever so carefully. Now my hands were really getting full. What a time to be without pockets. Yet, broken glass in pockets… not a good idea.

Last but not least, at approximately 4 miles into the walk, I passed by an old cemetery. On the road near the gated entrance, I got my final blue something. As with the other objects – it was right in front of me. Bright blue ear plugs connected with a bright blue string. I laughed out loud at that one. I could almost hear God say… *Time to get those plugs out of your ears. Listen to Me.*

Throughout the last stretch of my morning walk, I'd look down at my hands filled with blue items that didn't seem the least bit connected. If the sum of them were a clue from God for direction in my life, I wasn't getting it. Not at all. However, I will say – it was great fun. Kind of like a treasure hunt, and I was smiling when I returned home. Definitely renewed. I even told my family about it and showed them the pieces. They didn't know what to make of my collection. I'm pretty sure they thought I was a bit crazy for picking up roadside trash. Regardless, I placed the blue stuff in a zip-lock baggie and tucked it away in my bedroom closet. If God gave me those objects for a reason, I'd have to wait on Him for the big reveal. His timing, not mine.

His word was in my heart
like a burning fire
shut up in my bones;
I was weary of holding it back,
And I could not.
Jeremiah 20:9 (NKJV)

This verse was read aloud at church. When I heard it, the Spirit of the Living God spoke to me... not in an audible voice. When God speaks, it's a deep assuredness that what I'm sensing/hearing/feeling – is from Him. So, what did He say after the verse was read? *Did you hear that? Did you REALLY hear that? What are you going to do about it? Hmmm???*

I could almost see Him standing in front of me, arms folded, drumming His fingers. I knew what He meant. It's probably not right to say that He's been hounding me about this for quite some time... but He has been. Relentlessly – honestly!

God has pursued me for 8 years to write a book about that darned old bag of blue stuff. It seemed such an odd request that I've tried to hide from it. I was confident that if this was something He wanted accomplished, He would be able to find another, more willing writer. Yet, that wasn't His plan because Jeremiah's words pierced me through and through. *I was weary of holding it back, and I could not.* I can relate to the anguish and weariness Jeremiah experienced from wrestling with God. However, I wasn't down for the count just yet, and the list of excuses began...

God, I don't have the time – our family is still crazy busy, and we have so many commitments already. *Really – who is the giver of time? I will make it possible.*

But what if this book doesn't come out the way You want it to? I don't want to disappoint You. *It will come out just right if you will trust Me to lead the way.*

But there was a really great Bible study by Priscilla Shirer that I wanted to participate in. It's called "Discerning the Voice of God." *You don't struggle with discerning My voice, but obedience – that's a different subject.*

Ouch. And so, trying my best to be obedient, we begin.

Dear friend, before we turn to the first chapter – let us speak heart to heart. It's important that you understand my motives. I am not sharing this rather odd story with you to puff myself up or to say – look how God speaks to me; see how special and unique I am. Nothing could be further from the truth, as God knows I'd prefer to hide from this project. I have certainly tried. But, with God, there is no place to hide. Therefore, I press on in my attempt to be obedient; hoping that my indwelling Spirit (the driving force behind this book) will <u>finally</u> give me peace. Please know that the experiences I share are simply meant to shed light on the profound love and guidance we receive from the Lord.

Lastly, know that <u>I am no saint</u>. I have made a lot of mistakes in my past, but thanks be to God through the shed blood of Jesus and the gift of confession – I am (and you are too) given a clean slate. We get up and try again. I am living proof that God can and will use the least of His people to reach the hearts of others. In doing so, He is glorified.

God the Father, God the Son and God the Holy Spirit – I give myself to you. Please use this empty vessel according to your good and holy will. Lead the way. Amen.

Optional:

Questions for Personal Growth or Small Group Discussion can be found on pages 89-111.

chapter 1

BLUE FLIP-FLOP

*Remove your sandals from your feet,
for the place where you stand is holy ground.
Exodus 3:5 (NABRE)*

When I asked God to give me a sign for some direction in my life, I can honestly say I didn't expect my first clue would be in the form of a blue flip-flop. Not a pair, mind you – just one. I can't decide if I was given the "flip" or the "flop." I lifted it up and examined it, then laughed when I realized it was my size. A right footed size 7. Rats – if only He'd given me both I could have worn them. With just one, the best I can do now is hop on one foot. So, if this blue flip-flop is from God, what is He trying to tell me? Just for fun, let's hop on over to the dictionary and see what we can find.

I knew the words *flip* <u>and</u> *flop* would be there, but I didn't think I'd be able to find them connected as in the object I was holding in my hands. But low and behold, the hyphenated version is right there in the *Merriam-Webster Dictionary* with the following definition…

Figure 4 On the road with God

FLIP-FLOP

: a type of loose rubber sandal

: a sudden change of opinion

My guess is God doesn't care what type of footwear I'm walking around in, but He does care about how I live my life. If He gave me a flip-flop, then I'm believing it's because He wants me to reflect on "a sudden change of opinion." And so, God leads, and I follow. He is leading me now to one of the best biblical flip-flop stories of all time. Let's read from the book of Acts chapter 9 verses 1 – 2. (By the way, if you don't have a Bible – now's a great time to get one!)

2

Saul, still breathing murderous threats against the disciples of the Lord, went to the high priest and asked him for letters to the synagogues in Damascus, that, if he should find any men or women who belonged to the Way (followers of Christ), he might bring them back to Jerusalem in chains.

Now comes the flip-flop. Let's fast forward to Acts 9:19-21 to witness <u>a sudden change of opinion</u>.

Saul stayed some days with the disciples in Damascus, and he began at once to proclaim Jesus in the synagogues, that <u>He is the Son of God</u>. All who heard him were astounded and said, "Isn't this the man who in Jerusalem ravaged those who call upon this name, and came here expressly to take them back in chains to the chief priests?"

Saul went from wanting to see the followers of Christ dead, to preaching that Christ is the Son of God! Wow!!! Is this something or what? <u>What</u> is the key word here! What in the world happened in those 17 verses that so radically changed Saul? In one word… Jesus. Saul had a life changing encounter with the Risen Lord.

On his journey, as he was nearing Damascus, a light from the sky suddenly flashed around him. He fell to the ground and heard a voice saying to him, "Saul, Saul, why are you persecuting me?" He said, "Who are you, sir?" The reply came, "I am Jesus, whom you are persecuting."
Acts 9:3-5

Jesus met Saul right where he was. An encounter so great, Saul couldn't deny Him. An encounter that transformed Saul from the inside out. A moment of conversion. Old to new. Dead to alive. That's the dash, you know. In our word f<u>lip-flop</u>, the dash represents the encounter with Christ. You can't get from the flip word to the flop word without passing through the dash first. Don't miss out on the dash.

The Samaritan woman at the well is another great example of a transformative dash experience. She had so much sin in her life she avoided other people as much as she could. When other women went to the well in the morning to fill their water jugs, she'd wait until the afternoon when it was scorching hot out. She knew others wouldn't be there then. She wanted to avoid their stares, their looks of disapproval, and above all, their whispers; hurtful gossip about her lifestyle.

One afternoon, in the heat of the day – someone was at the well, waiting for her. Jesus. That encounter stirs me to tears every time. It's such a tender story and it can be found in John 4. I love that Jesus had a divine appointment with her; one He wouldn't miss. His relationship with her was THAT IMPORTANT. Our relationship with Him is THAT important too. Despite the fact that she was knee deep in sin, He forgave her, and she was the very first person He revealed His true identity to.

Can I just tell you something? There is no better place to start this book than to reflect on our relationship with Christ. What is yours like? Do you know Jesus? I mean, really KNOW Him. Yes? Maybe? No? If you are on the fence, then please stay tuned because in Chapter 4 we'll be going for a ride in my little time machine built for two (you and me) to visit February 23, 1998. The day THIS (me) walking-dead person had an encounter with our Living God, my personal "dash" experience – but for now let's wrap up with Saul. His story is amazing.

Saul, better known as the Apostle Paul (Acts 13:9), was literally brought to his knees before he changed his life and surrendered it to Christ. Apparently while he was kneeling, he miraculously underwent a heart transplant. Because, when he stood back up, his zealous, condemning heart had been replaced with a compassionate, obedient servant's heart.

Does it strike you as odd that God would use a man like this to blaze a trail through Christian history that many of us have followed? God does this frequently throughout scripture and it drives a message home. That message is this... God uses people you'd least expect to draw other's closer to Him. People with a past, who have sinned against Him and repented... they have great stories of redemption to share. They are relatable and give us hope. Because none of us are perfect, all have sinned and fallen short of the goal. This all-important sharing transforms our shame into goldens keys that unlock the doors of hope in other people's lives. If unconfessed sin is holding you back, the Lord is closer to you than you think.

The Lord is near to those who have a broken heart,
and saves such as have a <u>contrite</u> spirit.
Psalm 34:18

Before we close this chapter, let's take a look at one more definition in Webster's Dictionary.

CONTRITE

: feeling or expressing remorse or penitence; affected by guilt

Is there a flip-flop needed in your life? Do you feel like you need to get something off your chest, a need to come clean, a little interior housekeeping? Time to take an inventory of all that weighs heavy on your Spirit.

A few years ago, I was committed to a deep cleansing of unconfessed sin. The little sins I confessed freely and was very ok with letting them go. It was the bigger sins, those hard to speak aloud, that I kept hidden away. They were always there – just below the surface, and I was determined to get rid of them once and for all.

I sat down with a piece of paper and wrote anything that I felt I hadn't confessed to God. It was an extensive soul searching; some of those sins went back to my childhood. Fifty plus years later, I still carried them with me. I wrongly believed I deserved to feel their painful reminders as a form of punishment – a very deserving punishment – for having committed them in the first place.

Oh – my dear friend, don't get caught in this trap. It's one of Satan's favorites. He wants us to be ashamed so we will keep our sin inside. He wants us to feel unworthy of God's love and forgiveness; to separate us from our Father. But please hear these words and take them to heart…

> *This is <u>real love</u>: not that we loved God, but that He loved us*
> *and sent His Son as a sacrifice to take away our sins.*
> *1 John 4:10*

Are you ready to receive REAL LOVE? Are you ready to let go of the baggage you've been carrying around? Are you ready to be made new? Let today be your day. Grab a sheet of paper and pen. Ask your Spirt to bring to mind any unconfessed sin (no matter how large or how small) and bravely write them down. Then confess them to God as soon as possible. Remember – confession is a sacred gift. Don't leave it unopened.

If you chose this path, slip off those flip-flops. You'll be standing on holy ground. The angels rejoice because the powers of darkness have been defeated, through the saving blood of Jesus. And, about that written list of past sins – burn it. They are forgiven, forgotten… GONE!

Blue Flip-Flop Treasure Takeaway:

Don't miss out on the dash – your personal encounter with the Risen Lord. Confession is a gift that leads to peace. A clear conscience makes a soft pillow.

Optional:

Questions for Personal Growth or Small Group Discussion can be found on page 92.

chapter 2
BLUE SPOON

You should clothe yourselves with the beauty that comes from within,
the unfading beauty of a gentle and quiet spirit, which is so precious to God.
1 Peter 3:4 (NLT)

Soon after the blue flip-flop, I saw a blue handled children's spoon on the ground. Treasure #2. *But why a spoon, God?* All I could think of was my granddaughter, Luna. She is my little sweet pea, my sunshine, and my first grandchild. When my daughter, Lindsey, had to return to work after having Luna – I had the great joy of watching her from the age of just 6 weeks old until she went to kindergarten. How I loved holding her, rocking her, even changing her diapers. I felt blessed, tired – yes, but overwhelmingly blessed. The blue handled spoon reminded me of mornings with Luna and the first few times I fed her soupy rice cereal from a baby spoon. *But is this what you want me to write about God?*

Sitting here now, I'm trying to figure out why He'd give me a spoon. Maybe He wants a story about the joy of being a grandparent or the wisdom that comes with age? Or how about – not eating from a dirty spoon; as in – be careful what we put into our minds? After all, the spoon I picked up was dirty! That could be an interesting spin on it. Or about feeding ourselves

God's Word. Nothing seemed just right. But it didn't take long before my Spirit began to sing. Not a song I would expect Him to sing but it's there, nonetheless. Want to hear it too?

> *A spoon full of sugar helps the medicine go down, the medicine go down… the medicine go down. Just a spoon full of sugar helps the medicine go down in a most delightful way.*[1]

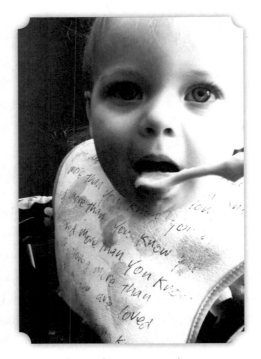

Figure 5 Luna, my sunshine

Remember that song from the 1964 film classic "Mary Poppins?" I love Mary Poppins! And that's some pretty good advice too. Let's see where this will go…

Have you ever tried to feed someone medicine from a fork? I have and let me tell you – it doesn't work well at all. Things get super messy, and the medicine typically ends up on the face of the one serving it and not in the mouth of the one who was supposed to receive it. There are two memories that "Poppins" to my head that I think demonstrate the need to use spoons. The first is a memory of my son, Ryan. I will share my fork mess afterwards.

Ryan was probably 7 or 8 years old at the time. He had his friend, Joey, over to the house so they could play together. Things got a little quiet, so I decided to check in on them. I was surprised at what I found. Ryan and Joey were sitting cross-legged on the floor having a deep conversation. Well... mostly all I heard was Ryan. As I drew closer, I could hear a bit of what he was saying... and it sounded like he was delivering a sermon to Joey.

Wide-eyed Joey sat there listening to things like; "if you want to be saved you have to believe in Jesus... Jesus is the only way to get into heaven." And... "we have to be sorry for our sins. Have you ever told God you're sorry when you do bad things?" I think Ryan wanted to make sure that his little friend would be with him in heaven one day. My guess is he had heard something at church (or maybe something I said). Only God knows. Ryan had good intentions, but his approach definitely wasn't from a soft spoon because Joey looked terrified. After he left, Ryan and I continued that discussion so we could both learn from it. Apparently, I had more learning to do. Shall we move onto my fork instead of spoon story? Mine is a bit longer.

My father-in-law, Harley, was in need of some medicine. He was very ill. No amount of prescription medications would bring about his physical healing. The kind of medication he needed was spiritual. The sicker he got, the more anxious he became because he feared death. Death was, in his view, the end. He had no expectation that heaven awaited him. As a

Jehovah's Witness, he believed in God, yet this faith allowed only a select few to pass through heaven's gates (144,000 to be exact) and he was certain he wasn't one of the chosen. He seemed hopeless and it hurt me to see it.

So, what does this daughter-in-law do? Grab a giant fork and a big bottle of spiritual medicine and head over to see Harley. I rapped on the back door of my in-law's home, then let myself in. My mother-in-law was the first to see me. She also saw that I was carrying a Bible. The look on her face spoke volumes… "Oh boy, here we go," it said.

I took a seat next to Harley at the dining room table – determined to pour out a big dose of medicine. "Harley," I said. "I know you believe in God, but you don't believe you will see heaven because you haven't been 'chosen.'" He had a look on his face that silently said the very same thing my mother-in-law's expression said… "Oh boy, here we go." Yet I continued.

"I read something this morning in the Bible," I said, "that I really want to share with you. I think it will give you some hope." I opened the bottle and forked out truth. Big, big doses of truth. When the dust settled, what I hoped to hear from him was… "I feel so much better." Instead, what Harley said to me was, "We have our differences, but we sure do love each other." That was a true statement, but not what I was hoping for. In the end, we agreed to disagree. That medicine did not go down in a most delightful way. Not at all.

When I left Harley, I didn't get the feeling that our talk had been fruitful. Yet there was always the hope that a few seeds of truth fell along his pathway toward inner peace and that God would help them grow. After all, with God all things are possible.

When a baby first begins to take nourishment beyond its mother's breast, it's typically rice cereal served from a very small and soft rubber tipped spoon. One would never contemplate serving an infant rice cereal from a fork. Likewise, when God nudges us to share a message of hope with others – we should use a soft spoon approach.

Two things come to mind. First... the "nudge." Second... the "spoon." Let's tackle the "nudge" first. When someone asks you a spiritual question, God is drawing them closer to Himself. He wants to give that person a physical touch – so He stirs within them until a question rises to the surface. This person might come to you after having noticed something about you that would lead them to believe you may have an answer – that's God's elbow to your side. *"Look here."* God says, *"I brought someone to you. They have a question that I'd like you to help them with so they can know Me better."*

Looking at my example of the fork method with Harley, he didn't invite me to come over. I knocked on the door and let myself in. He and Nancy didn't even have a chance to come to the door. By the time they heard the knock, I was already in the dining room with Bible in hand. They didn't open the door, I pushed it open. Nor did Harley ask any spiritual questions that would lead me to believe God had invited me to join Him in His work. He didn't say, "I'm afraid to die because I don't believe heaven awaits me. Would you help me find truth on this so I can rest in peace?" In hindsight, I should have waited for that all-important nudge from God. This wasn't God's timing, it was mine.

Now – onto the importance of choosing the right spoon for the job. The soft spoon helps this beautiful life-saving medicine go down. Saint Teresa of Calcutta perfectly defined this gentle way to feed others when she said... *"Spread the love of God through your life, but only use words when necessary."* Can we just rewind and play that one more time – because this is really, REALLY important. "Spread the love of God THROUGH YOUR LIFE, but <u>only use words</u> WHEN NECESSARY." What does that mean? It means to live your life in a manner that honors the One who gave you life. In doing so, others may see a glimpse of God through you.

Back to Harley – in the end, I believe he knew more about my faith in God by my actions than by my words. And those seeds that I hoped God would nurture and grow… well, they eventually did fall on fertile soil. Nancy's soil. Not long after Harley passed, my mother-in-law, just shy of 80 years old, chose to leave the Jehovah's Witness faith to become a Catholic. She hungered to know and love Jesus through the Eucharist. At the age of 90, she continues to live her faith and serves God with great joy, singing in the choir.

Can we do another rewind/replay? *Harley didn't invite me to come over. I knocked on the door and let myself in. He and Nancy didn't even have a chance to come to the door. By the time they heard the knock, I was already in the dining room with Bible in hand. They didn't open the door, I pushed it open.* How would Jesus have done this differently? Well, one of Jesus' most endearing qualities is that He's a gentleman. He waits to be invited into our lives.

> *Jesus said, "Behold, I stand at the door and knock. If anyone hears my voice and opens the door, I will enter his house and dine with him, and he with me. I will give the victor the right to sit with me on my throne, as I myself first won the victory and sit with my Father on his throne."*
> *Revelation 3:20-21 (NABRE)*

There's a famous painting that embodies our *gentleman Jesus* by William Holman Hunt entitled *The Light of the World*. He created it in 1851 and it is one of the most viewed 20th century art pieces in the world. It is considered by many to be the most important rendering of Christ of its time. In fact, it's often referred to as a "sermon in a frame" because of its rich tapestry of symbolism.

I would like to take a moment to describe to you this stunning painting (you might want to go on-line and search for it so you can see it for yourself). It's night. Jesus is standing in front of an old wooden door. There are vines and weeds growing against the door; it appears it hasn't been opened in quite some time. Some believe the weeds represent sin that separates us from Jesus and the closed door represents the obstinately shut mind. In His left hand, He is holding a lantern from which a radiant light pours forth, illuminating His gown, face, crown, and the door. With His right hand he is knocking on the door. It has no handle on the outside. Jesus can't open it; it must be opened by the person on the inside of the home. The expression on Jesus' face is one of patient determination.

If I could use anything to illustrate the "gentle feeding, soft spoon approach," this painting is perfect. JESUS IS THE GREAT PHYSICIAN SERVING MEDICINE FROM A GENTLE SPOON. He healed many people, body, mind, and spirit. He continues to bring healing today. He gently knocks at our heart's door. He doesn't open it Himself, barge into our lives demanding us to change. No – he waits patiently to be invited in. When He knocks, do we open the door to Him, or do we pretend that we don't hear His knock? Do we hear the knock but are afraid to answer the door because of all the weeds (sin) that block the entrance to the door?

Dear one, don't miss the gentle knock on the door. Don't be afraid to open it when you hear it, because the nail pierced hand that's doing the knocking already paid the price for our sins. If you will open the door, Jesus will come into your life and "dine" with you, He will partake with you as a friend. And isn't that what our hearts are most hungry for?

Blue Spoon Treasure Takeaway:

Use the soft-spoon approach. Help others know God through your life; use words only when necessary. And, above all – if you hear a gentle knock on your door be sure to open it.

Optional:

Questions for Personal Growth or Small Group Discussion can be found on page 94.

chapter 3

BLUE LIGHTER

In my distress I called to the Lord;
I cried to my God for help.
From His temple He heard my voice;
my cry came before Him, into His ears.
Psalm 18:6 (NIV)

A blue lighter… I reached down and picked it up, then rolled my finger over the spark wheel. Instantly it brought forth a flame. It surprised me that it still worked because it wasn't in great shape. I don't know why but seeing that flame made me happy. Maybe it's because it had fallen to the wayside but was still very useful. Strange as it may seem, I can relate to that lighter. Maybe you can too. The feeling of wanting to be useful despite past circumstances and mistakes. I longed to be useful to others, most importantly to be found useful to God. I believe that longing is what opened the door to the most profound experience I have had with Him.

Spring of 2012 – Mary Ethel Eckard (whom you met in the Introduction of this book) was a guest speaker at a Christian conference for women.

The conference was being held just a few hours away in Pennsylvania, so I decided to make the drive there. I hadn't seen Mary in quite a while as she lived in Maryland at the time. So, when she got a break between programs, we had an opportunity to catch up.

One of the conversations we had turned toward women's retreats. I shared with her that I had an idea for a retreat but wasn't sure if it was something I wanted or if it was something God was leading me to plan. In a nutshell, I explained that my vision was for an "Extreme Retreat for Women." One where we would be challenged physically and spiritually, with a great speaker and Bible teacher (that's where Mary would come in). A retreat that provided some time for quiet reflection; an opportunity to hear from God apart from the distractions in life. The location would be the Adirondack mountains. The physical challenge would be to climb Mount Marcy – the highest peak in New York State. It would be a day hike 16 miles long. And having done the hike before, I knew how hard it was. Participants would really need to be up for that kind of physical challenge.

As we were speaking, a woman I didn't know leaned toward me. She said, "I'm sorry for eavesdropping, but if you ever decide to do that retreat, please let me know. I would love to join you." She wrote down her name and phone number on a slip of paper and gave it to me. Turns out, her name was Liz. After she left, Mary and I looked at each other and said, I guess we're having an Extreme Retreat. Our first participant just signed up.

The planning began. So many details. From food, to gear, to the message Mary would deliver during the retreat. In my mind, I saw us gathering Friday evening for part 1 of Mary's talk. Saturday would be "hike day," followed by a celebration dinner for having conquered the mountain. Sunday morning we'd have a breakfast of champions, attend church, then Mary would do part 2 of her talk before we'd say good-bye and return home. Oh, the vision I had of us gathering together on the mountain top. I couldn't wait for the weekend God was preparing for us.

Let's fast forward to hike day. We were at the trailhead at 6:30 a.m. Excitement was in the air. We took pictures of each other signing in on the register at the trailhead, with name and time. This is routine on most trails. Park staff check the register in the evening to make sure everyone signed back out. So, there we were, 13 ladies all lined up for one last photo before heading out. Well, 13 ladies and my dad. He didn't want to miss out on the adventure. At almost 78, climbing Marcy was on his bucket list, and we were thrilled to have him join us. Mom came too – but not to hike. She would stay behind making her amazing spaghetti sauce for our celebration dinner, and to support us in prayer.

Figure 6 Hikers from the Extreme Retreat Weekend

There's an old saying, "man plans, and God laughs." And so it was. I envisioned us all hiking together like little ducks in a row. We'd reach the summit together and share a truly remarkable moment, with a great view celebrating God's wonderous creation. Mary would speak a few words, and we'd head back down and celebrate some more. But my vision wasn't meant to be.

Soon after we started the trek, the hikers quickly broke down into little groups of their own accord. We had two super-fast walkers who shot out of the gates. Next came two ladies who weren't far behind them. Half a mile down the trail was a group of four who were moving at a fairly good pace. A couple of switchbacks below them were two ladies who had been best friends since kindergarten. Lastly, our group of four. I'd say we were the "taking our own sweet time so we don't get hurt" hikers. Dad and I stayed at the end of this foursome.

In my perfect planning, I never anticipated our group separating, hence I didn't give each lady a trail map. Big mistake. At present, my little ducks were EVERYWHERE, and it frightened me. People can get lost in this wilderness. One of the few things I DID do right was to give each one a whistle in case of emergency, as cell service is almost non-existent. I thought, at the very least, if we got separated and couldn't communicate in time of need, there was the hope that we'd hear the sound of a whistle.

Would you believe we heard a whistle blowing? My heart sank. As we got closer, we found the two best friends. One was blowing a whistle because they thought they were lost. There had been a split in the trail, and they lost sight of the trail markers. We were all relieved to find each other. They joined our group and we pressed on. Together we (six now) moved ever so slowly toward the peak. I had no idea where the rest of the group was. I prayed God was protecting them.

We climbed the last bit to the summit. It was enshrouded in fog, and like a veil, it separated us from the grand view that I had hoped we'd all share together. The only things we saw were big black ravens flying low around us and several rock cairns left by other hikers over the years. A cairn is a stack of rocks that folks build to commemorate something. That was part of my vision as well. I thought it would be so cool if our entire group gathered on the summit and built a cairn together honoring our God and our shared experience. That was my plan, but God's plan was radically different as a storm was coming and coming fast.

Lightning was a major worry when standing on a bald summit in a storm 5,300 feet above sea level. We didn't take time to enjoy reaching the peak, instead we set our sights on the long trek back to camp. Did I say long? Oh, my goodness… long. Our caboose group moved much slower on the return trip. We couldn't move fast. Those boulder infested trails had become streams of running water, but we pressed on.

Back to my planning vision. Because I'd climbed Marcy before, I anticipated us returning to camp around 5 p.m. Maybe 6 at the latest. That was even padded with extra time, but I never anticipated moving as slowly as we were. And we were slow moving for a myriad of reasons. One reason, we had an injury coming down the mountain. One of our hikers hurt her knee badly. Also, the rocks had become super slippery, and we ran into mud. What else could go wrong? How about extreme exhaustion! Really sore toes! Cramping muscles! Approaching darkness! Lions and tigers and bears – oh my.

Did I mention darkness approaching? *Oh, Lord, not the darkness.* We arrived at Marcy Dam and had about 2 ½ miles to go. By now, my physical exhaustion was surpassed greatly by my emotional exhaustion. Being the organizer of the "Extreme Retreat" in addition to the backpack I carried, I was also carrying a great burden on my shoulders. I felt completely responsible for everyone's exhaustion, their scrapes, bruises, injured knee and now – we'd be hiking in the darkness, and I didn't even know where half the crew was. And the prince of darkness was in my ear. *"You fool,"* he said. *"Who do you think you are? You are a joke! Look at you – the great retreat planner, dragging your people through the mud."* If I could have crawled under a rock, I would have. It was an extreme retreat alright. An extreme FAILURE!

Before leaving Marcy Dam, I did two things. First, I pulled out my cell phone and turned it on. I knew there wouldn't be cell service but, just in case it broke through, I'd keep the phone handy because I knew my husband (John), my mom, and others would be frantic that we hadn't yet returned. We should have been back by now. I tried to call John but no surprise – the call didn't go through. No service. The second thing I did was to ask everyone to pull out the headlamps they were supposed to pack. Guess what? Not many brought them. Great. Now we'd be on the last leg of our hike walking in treacherous conditions with almost no light. What next, God?

What do you do in this situation? The only thing I knew I could do. I prayed. In silence, I literally poured my heart out to God, in the rawest form. I pleaded with Him. *GOD HELP US!* Just then, my phone rang. I was shocked to hear it and dreaded the idea of answering it. I didn't want to have to explain to anyone the situation we were in because of shame. Yet I said, "Hello." I was not prepared for what I heard next. It sounded like a recorded message with a voice I wasn't familiar with. And this is EXACTLY what was spoken… VERBATIM!

> *Hello – I hear you are in trouble. God has heard your prayers. If you would like to speak with someone to pray with you through this difficult time, press 1 now."*

What??? I almost fell on the ground. I did not press 1. I put my phone down in complete awe. What? How? I cried. God HAD heard my prayers, and I KNEW IT. I never had a call like that before and haven't had one since that day, Saturday, August 11, 2012. After that call, other calls came in. First John, trying to find out where we were. He had called the forest rangers to report us still on the trail and to be watching for us. Next, my brother, Jim, called, and he wasn't very happy that we were still out there hiking – especially since Dad had issues with his heart. Jim said he would call off the "search party" when he found out we had under three miles to go.

It was 10:30 p.m. when we finally reached the sign-in log at the trailhead. I quickly looked at all the names and times of when our crew returned. Thanks be to God all had signed off. All were accounted for. With that, we piled into our van and drove back to camp. Mom and those who had returned earlier had been praying for us. When we walked through the door, they cheered. I went straight to my bedroom, fell on the floor, and wept. All home safe and sound – minus a few bumps, bruises, lots of aches and pains, and one injured knee. Each with a story to tell of God's faithfulness. A hike that won't be forgotten.

Like the Samaritan woman after meeting Jesus at the well, I told everyone I could about that hike and the "phone call from God." I mean EVERYONE!!! And most everyone asked me the same question. Why didn't you press #1 and see who you were connected with when you got that call? In hindsight I believe I didn't because I didn't need to speak with another human being. From the bottom of my heart, in the depths of my knowing, I believe it was God responding to my plea for help in the clearest, most tangible way I've ever experienced. God is real. God hears our prayers. And I believe He gave me that experience because He knew I would tell that story at every opportunity. Just like I'm telling it again now, and to share a message of hope: *His light shines greatest in the darkness.*

In the darkness… when my oldest two children were quite young, I took them to a place called Inner Space not far from Austin, Texas to explore underground caverns. The thing that stands out most in my memory about that visit is this. In the midst of the caverns, stalactites and stalagmites, our guide said: "In a minute we are going to turn off all of the lights down here so you can experience perfect darkness." Soon afterwards, the lights went out. There was absolute nothingness. You couldn't see your hand in front of your face. It was freaky and I'm pretty sure I wasn't alone in thinking *what if the lights don't come back on – how will we find our way out.* A little feeling of panic followed. But just then, our guide lit a match. A single little match. And would you believe that tiny light filled the vast cavern we were standing in?

And so, God lit the way for us on our hike – like that little match through the darkness, back to our camp, back to warmth, food and a nice hot shower, with stories of His faithfulness throughout our journey. Stories that each of us would need to illuminate steppingstones of faith in the days ahead; for days when we needed something firm to stand on.

> *Because he loves me, says the Lord, I will rescue him;*
> *I will protect him, for he acknowledges my name.*
> *He will call on me, and <u>I will answer him</u>;*
> *I will be with him in trouble, I will deliver and honor him.*
> *With long life I will satisfy him and show him my salvation.*
> *Psalm 91:14-16 (NIV)*

<u>Blue Lighter Treasure Takeaway</u>:

God hears our prayers. He is our ever-present light in the darkness.

<u>Optional:</u>

Questions for Personal Growth or Small Group Discussion can be found on page 96.

chapter 4
BLUE PEN

For the word of God is alive and powerful.
It is sharper than the sharpest two-edged sword,
cutting between the soul and spirit, between the joint and marrow.
It exposes our innermost thoughts and desires.
Hebrews 4:12 (NLT)

The blue pen lay at my feet. God's fourth treasure on my hunt. This is one piece of the puzzle that I thought I knew the meaning of as soon as I picked it up. Write. Writing is something I haven't done in a very long time, and I suspected God was telling me to get back to doing that. So here I am writing today about the blue pen, all set to jump into the deep waters of spiritual gifts. About what I believe is my gift, and about what you can do to discover and apply yours, yet the Holy Spirit speaks. *Whoa! Not so fast! Who's steering this ship anyway?* Feeling confused, I paused. A pen seemed the easiest of my pieces of blue treasure to figure out. I was certain it had to do with spiritual gifts. After all, that made the most sense. Yet, my good teacher (Spirit) reminds me of the following verses from Isaiah.

For my thoughts are not your thoughts,
nor are your ways my ways, says the Lord.
As the heavens are higher than the earth,
so are my ways higher than your ways
and my thoughts above your thoughts.
Isaiah 55:8-9 (NCB)

God's ways are higher than my ways. His thoughts higher than my thoughts. That's for sure. I decided to tuck this away for another day. He's the captain of this ship. I'm just here for the ride.

I'm back. Turns out I was closer than I realized. The word "captain" tipped me off.

March 2023 – Bonita Springs, Florida. I was visiting my snow-bird parents in their little home. When I say little, envision a 1970s Airstream trailer with a Florida room attached to it. Mom and Dad referred to their home as "the silver bullet." When we stepped inside, it was a blast from the past with the original galley kitchen, twin beds on either side of the narrow hallway leading to the tiniest bathroom ever. Mom had a bed in the nose of the trailer; the original foldout couch. She liked to sleep there because of the big window along the bedside where she could look up at the night sky. Dad slept in one of the twin beds; the one on the right side of the land yacht, to be exact. Whenever a family member stayed with them, we'd usually sleep in the extra twin bed across from dad.

On this particular trip, I was settling into my bed with Dad an arm's length away in his bed. I turned on my side and saw him with pen in hand, writing in a small notebook. This was no ordinary notebook. My entire family knows exactly what it is; his "captain's journal." So named by the "captain" himself. Each night before he falls asleep, he puts a few thoughts down on paper. Maybe today's entry was about a task completed, or about a bird or alligator he spotted at Trost Pond. Whatever the case, this has been a part of his nightly routine for many years. When one notebook fills up, he starts another. After the day's entry has been made, the captain spends time in prayer, often reading Scripture.

That night as I watched Dad write in his dimly lit berth – a thought occurred to me. One day when he's passed from this life into eternity, he will live on through our memories of him and his captain's journals. Those little notes about random things and thoughts will mean the world to us. Until then, we won't know what the pages contain.

Figure 7 The Captain

Do you know that our Almighty Captain, God, has a stack of journals He wrote for us too? There are approximately 70 of them and they are better known as the "Books of the Bible." When combined, they make up the Bible. God gave some forty plus dedicated servants the words to each of those books. And, through those words, He shares His heart, His truth, His love, His wisdom and His guidance with us. Shouldn't we then take the time to read those books – as they come from Wisdom Himself? When we are in trouble, when we are lost or confused, when we are afraid, when we need comfort, when we are in whatever the day brings – if we turn to His Word, God will lead the way. His Truth will calm the storms. His Truth will give us what we need so we can get our feet back on solid ground.

Maybe it would be helpful if we had an example of how this works. Let's say we are struggling with faith. There was a man named Thomas who had some doubts too. He found it hard to believe that Jesus really rose from the dead. Let's turn to one of God's "captain's journals" to see what happened. This particular "journal" is entitled *John*.

> *One of the disciples, Thomas, was not with the others when Jesus*
> *came. They told him, "We have seen the Lord!" But he replied, "I*
> *won't believe it unless I see the nail wounds in his hands, put my*
> *fingers into them, and place my had into the wound in his side."*
> *John 20:24-25 (NLT)*

Have you ever felt like Doubting Thomas? Wanting to believe but just needing something you could physically touch. Hard evidence that all of these eggs you are carrying around in one basket are in the right basket to begin with? Well Jesus knows that our beautiful souls are wrapped in human skin. Because He wore the same skin. We strive to do what is right, but unlike Him we sometimes fall short of the goal. Thomas stumbled in faith, but Jesus helped him to his feet in a very intimate way.

Eight days later the disciples were together again, and this time Thomas was with them. The doors were locked; but suddenly, as before, Jesus was standing among them. He said, "Peace be with you. Then he said to Thomas, "Put your finger here and see my hands. Put your hand into the wound in my side. Don't be faithless any longer. Believe!" My Lord and my God! Thomas exclaimed. Then Jesus told him, "You believe because you have seen me. Blessed are those who haven't seen me and believe anyway."
John 20:26-29 (NLT)

Jesus gave Thomas a gift that was uniquely his – literally a hands-on experience (his "dash" encounter) that would become Thomas' faith stone. Something to stand on when his faith would be tested again. We all need a faith stone to stand on. As another example of this faith stone – I'd like to share mine with you. Which leads us to our ride in the time machine I promised back in Chapter 1. It's pulling up to the curb right now...

The hatch is open -- welcome aboard! Our destination is set for February 23, 1998 – The Colony, Texas. This was a bumpy season in my life; for your safety, please remain seated with your seatbelt securely fastened around your waist. Place your tray in its upright position and ensure that your bag is stowed away in the overhead compartment. Away we go...

The bumpy season I mentioned didn't just occur during the month of February 1998, nor was it spread out over the course of the year before. I'd say it began somewhere around 20 years earlier when I was 18 years old and oh-so-wise -- NOT! A little bad decision here, a little bad decision there. Then here, there, and everywhere. Until I crash landed. Speaking of landed... here we are. It's 3 a.m. We are in my home and I'm crying like a baby at the dining room table. Another of those bad decisions had reared its ugly head. My crying turned into big ugly sobs from a guttural place deep inside. Yes, because of the situation, but also because I felt utterly alone. I had moved to Texas from New York many years earlier, so I didn't have a family member nearby. Nor did I have a close friend that I felt I could confide in about the situation.

In the months leading up to this crisis, I was very new to reading from the Bible. I can't remember why I ever picked it up to begin with. Perhaps it could only be explained as divine intervention. Whatever the reason, I found that I couldn't put it down. My heart was hungry for the *Living Word of God*. And what did that mean anyway? That *"Living"* part?! I was about to discover exactly what that meant! I cried out to Him…

God – if you are real, I need to know. Please. I NEED YOU! My life is a mess, and I am completely alone. My family is so far away, and I have no one here. Please comfort me. Please… PLEASE COMFORT ME! I need YOUR COMFORT!!!

Now was the moment of truth. I took hold of the Bible. At random, I stuck my finger into the pages and flipped it open. Here are the first words I saw:

WORDS OF COMFORT

"Comfort, comfort my people," says your God.
Isaiah 40:1 (NIV)

I, like Thomas, fell at Christ's feet and humbly said *"My Lord and my God!"* I had pleaded with God to comfort me, and He gave me exactly what I asked for. He wrapped His arms around me through the pages of the Bible. As I read the chapter, God led me into a deeper understanding of my "crisis" situation and how to navigate it. He also brought me to the verse that became my life verse, *"The grass withers, and the flowers fade, but the Word of our God stands forever"* Isaiah 40:8.

Several years later, I was reading "my" Bible (the one that God used to speak to me on 2/23/98) and a thought occurred. I wondered what the very first printed words in it were. Were they a list of the books of the Bible? Publishing information? An introduction? No. Not even close. Hang onto your seat because the very first words printed in my Bible are:

The grass withers, and the flowers fade,
but the Word of our God stands forever.
Isaiah 40:8 (NLT)

Humbly I fell at Christ's feet again and said, *"My Lord and my God!"* I believe God wanted me to have a very special something to remind me of that early morning "dash" experience with Him. The unique moment in time when the God of the Universe came to me at my dining room table. Even today, when I read that verse inside my Bible cover, I see His seal of authenticity. His autograph.

God wants YOU to know Him too.

He created YOU from the dust.
He loved YOU into being.
He sacrificed all for YOU.
He guides YOU in safety along life's journey.
He shields YOU from the powers of darkness.
He offers YOU everlasting life.
His seal of authenticity is on YOU.
He created YOU to be UNIQUELY YOU.
He gave YOU fingerprints unlike anyone else.
YOUR relationship with Him will be uniquely YOURS.

(All of these truths are documented in the
Bible, your "Captain's Journal.")

31

Before our time machine leaves Texas, I'd like to make one last quick stop. There's a community rummage sale going on. I can't resist a good rummage sale. Jackpot. I needed books. My home had an office area with lots of empty shelves begging for some books. Before me now were paper bags chocked full of old books and they were just $2 a bag. They weren't divided into various reading genres, you just got what you got. I took two bags home and began placing them on the shelves.

In one of the bags, I came across a Bible with a worn leather cover. Inside a name was written: Dorothy Owen. I began to flip through the pages and discovered that, while I never met Dorothy nor had a clue who she was, I knew something about her. She loved God's Word! Page after page of her beloved Bible had been touched by her. Using pens, pencils, and markers, she made that Bible her own. In countless margins she wrote notes. Verse after verse she underlined truths. Perhaps they were moments God spoke to her as she read. As I closed Dorothy's Bible, I wondered how one of her greatest treasures wound up in a rummage sale bag. It made me sad, yet grateful it found its way to my home.

My hope for you and for me is that one day, long after we are gone from this earth, someone will find our Bibles. When they do, let them find our hearts entwined with God's. Just as Dorothy's was. Let them find pages lovingly worn; verses underlined and margins written in – so they know that we, too, loved God's Word.

Well, my friend, let's make our way to the time machine. Can't leave you stranded at a rummage sale in Texas. Back to the present we go.

Do you know that Scripture is one of the ways God speaks with us? If we don't open the Bible, we are missing out on hearing His voice. If you haven't read from it recently, or never opened it before – there's no time like the present. Consider saying a little prayer before you do. Something like this… *"Come Holy Spirit. Lead me into a deeper understand of God's Word."* Then, take out your pen and do as Dorothy did; underline verses, write in the margins and document your personal encounter with the King of Kings.

The grass withers and the flowers fade,
but the WORD of our GOD stands <u>forever</u>."
Isaiah 40:8 (NLT)

<u>Blue Pen Treasure Takeaway</u>:

God speaks to us through the Bible. He loves you – <u>uniquely</u> you! Believe.

<u>Optional:</u>

Questions for Personal Growth or Small Group Discussion can be found on page 98.

chapter 5

BLUE BROKEN GLASS

The Lord heals the brokenhearted and binds up their wounds.
Psalm 147:3 (NKJV)

S hards of cobalt blue broken glass lay scattered on the pavement. The sunlight made them sparkle. I'd already picked up the other blue items on my journey so, naturally, I couldn't leave them behind simply because I didn't want to risk getting cut. I just needed to be careful; picking up one fragment at a time.

One fragment at a time. Try as I might, I could not get the blasted glue to hold. Frustration was mounting! Whose idea was this anyway? Oh yeah, right... mine. The idea was a craft project of sorts. You see, I had a beautiful lead crystal vase that had broken. Instead of tossing it into the trash, I thought it might be fun to try to create something useful from the pieces, and the "Broken Vase Project" came to be.

I carefully placed the larger pieces in a double paper bag, took a hammer, and broke them into smaller pieces. Next, I divided them into two small boxes. I put a note inside one box outlining the project challenge, then I got in the car and drove to my friend's house. I left the box at her front door. Maybe Michelle would be up for the challenge too. When I returned home, I went straight to work.

Have you ever tried to glue two pieces of broken glass together? Especially, heavy lead glass? If so, then you know how hard it is. I tried craft glue, epoxy glue, Gorilla glue, super glue... nothing worked well. At best, the pieces held together briefly, then slid apart before drying. The only things that seemed to stick together were my fingertips.

Eventually, I found a glue specifically for glass that worked so-so. Trying to be artsy – I formed the crystal pieces into an opened rose bud, although I'm not sure my family recognized it as such. It was definitely not something I'd place on our fireplace mantel to display, but the job was done. Task completed. I wondered how Michelle's effort was coming along.

Michelle took a while before attempting her reconstruction job. The box sat untouched for quite a while. Eventually, she opened it and began the same tedious process of connecting pieces. She, too, couldn't find a glue that worked well. Thinking the project was overwhelming, she nearly threw the pieces away until she thought of her young daughter, Sadie, who had a passion for duct tape. Yes... duct tape! She had a collection of it in various colors and designs because she used it to decorate all sorts of things; from notebook covers to picture frames. You name it, Sadie probably tried to stick duct tape to it.

So, Michelle borrowed a roll from Sadie. She placed a strip between two pieces, and, to her amazement, they held together. She added more pieces and more tape. A lot more tape. In the end, she'd made a new, very small vase that even held water without leaking. It didn't look anything like the original crystal vase. It wasn't necessarily a thing of beauty, yet it was beautiful to Michelle because it made her think of Sadie. In my estimation, Michelle took the win because, not only was her project useful, but it was also sentimental.

Figure 8 Michelle's broken vase project

Unbeknownst to us, I recently discovered that Michelle and I were dabbling in a true art form. We weren't doing it correctly, yet the idea is the same. It's called "Kintsugi." In 15th century Japan, according to legend, shogun Ashikago Yoshimasa broke his favorite ceramic tea bowl. He sent it out for repair. It was fixed and returned, but the repair was bound by ugly, metal staples. This inspired him to find an elegant way to restore ceramic, and the art of Kintsugi was born.

The name is derived from the words "Kin" (golden) and "tsugi" (joinery), which translated means "golden repair." The cracks, the scars of the broken pottery, are held together with a thin line of golden lacquer and turns broken objects into something unique, exquisite, and useful.

Can we revisit that last statement again? The CRACKS, the SCARS of the BROKEN pottery are held together with a thin line of golden lacquer and TURNS THE BROKEN OBJECTS INTO something UNIQUE, EXQUIST and USEFUL.

Let's go to the book of Jeremiah to read about another artisan skilled in pottery.

> *I went down to the potter's house, and I saw him working at the wheel.*
> *But the pot he was shaping from the clay was <u>marred</u> in his hands;*
> *so the potter formed it into <u>another pot</u>, shaping it <u>as seemed best to him</u>.*
> *Jeremiah 18:3-4 (NIV)*

Who is the potter described in these verses? God. Who is He working on at His pottery wheel? You and me. What is he trying to do? He's fixing what is broken; reshaping us to make us useful. Does He do this according to our wishes? No – He rebuilds us according to His good and holy will.

Do those tender words from Jeremiah touch your heart? They do mine. Tears of joy fall because of this truth: NOTHING is wasted with God. Not one single shard of glass. Not a single teardrop. He uses it all and turns those pieces into something UNIQUE, EXQUISITE and USEFUL. Shaping them as it seems best to Him. There are no better hands to be in.

How about a real-life example of this process?

<u>John's Broken Glass</u>

It was John and Stacy's fifth wedding anniversary when they received the sad news that Stacy had cancer. Further testing revealed it was widespread. They had a beautiful marriage and three precious children (an infant and two toddlers). Despite all life-saving efforts and the prayers of countless family members and friends, on July 25, 2006, Stacy passed from this life into the arms of Jesus.

The days that followed were a blur for John. He grieved. He made funeral arrangements. He grieved. He took the kids to daycare, and he bought groceries. He grieved and went to work; cleaned the house and mowed the grass. Life was not easy. He was in survival mode. Joy was missing. Stacy was missing.

That emptiness caused him to reach out to a co-worker. A relationship quickly ensued, but it didn't last. Yet there was a lasting result from it – a beautiful baby girl was born. His fourth child; a gift sent from heaven above.

However, if John's life was hard after Stacy passed, now it had become both hard and complex. Pieces were scattered all around him. He didn't know how to assemble them, but he trusted God did.

Patty's Broken Glass

My past made me feel unworthy of love, yet I continued to look for it. As a divorced woman with two children, I didn't think another man would find me worth the effort to pursue. Well, someone did, but not the right someone. I jumped from the fire into the frying pan and remarried. Turned out to be an abusive relationship; unsafe for myself and my kids. Divorce number two.

If I felt unworthy of love before, I was ever so unworthy now. In my estimation, I had become a two-time loser. Yet God, in His infinite love, met me in my brokenness. I discovered that what I needed wasn't the love of a man; I desperately needed to know HIS love.

That empty void that each of us are born with, that we fill with all sorts of things, can only be filled by Him. It wasn't until I came to know this fully that I was restored. Through deep soul searching, confession, and the help of my Church… our Heavenly Father gave me a clean slate. I was forgiven by God. I was a new creation and I finally felt worthy of His love and the love of others.

God's Golden Joinery

A few years after Stacy passed, John's friends invited him to a dance at church. It was an annual event called "The Hooley" (Irish for "party in the kitchen") and it was typically held just before Saint Patrick's Day. The Hooley was always well attended. The crowd danced to Irish music. There was food, fun and festivities.

A friend invited me to go as well, but that particular year I didn't want to go. She bought me a ticket anyway as a birthday gift – so I went to please her. When we arrived, I stood along the wall, I didn't dance or even take my coat off. My goal was to stay 30 minutes then go home. Before I could leave, I noticed another friend heading toward me. He wanted to introduce me to a "nice man" he knew. I wasn't interested. Not at all. But he kept pleading with me, saying "just come over and say hello." I gave in so he'd stop badgering me. He introduced me to John.

John's first words to me were, "I have little kids, does that scare you?" I responded, "I have big kids, does that scare you?" John extended his hand and invited me to dance. I took the hand he offered, and he led me to the dancefloor. As we began to dance, I can only explain it like this… it felt as if the crowd around us had disappeared and it was just the two of us dancing alone. We both experienced that.

John and I have been married now for almost 15 years. We have a great big beautifully blended family. Eight pieces brought together by God Himself; as it seemed best to Him. Does that mean things are perfect all the time? No - and that's okay, because we are all perfectly-imperfect people. We are a real family, with real ups and downs, joys, squabbles, laughter and tears. Yet through it all, He IS our glue...the golden joinery that holds our pieces together in a most glorious way.

Back to Michelle. Michelle wasn't eager to jump right into our project, or even ready to open the box of broken glass. She was in a place of profound brokenness herself. A few months prior to this, she experienced a loss so big she didn't know where to go with the pain. Her beloved cousin, Christina, and Christina's friend (Mario) had been brutally murdered. Michelle was shattered; like tiny bits of cobalt blue glass scattered on the ground. But God didn't leave them there. He tenderly collected each little fragment, each teardrop, and is at work, even now, rebuilding what was broken.

If you are in the midst of a broken season, cling to your faith. You are not alone. Trust that God is near, you are in His hands, on His wheel – being reshaped. Restoration will take place – in His perfect timing and in His perfect way.

> *We are pressed on every side by troubles, but we are not crushed.*
> *We are perplexed, but not driven to despair.*
> *We are hunted down, but never abandoned by God.*
> *We get knocked down, but we are not destroyed.*
> *Through suffering, our bodies continue to share in the death of Jesus*
> *so that the life of Jesus may also be seen in our bodies.*
> *2 Corinthians 4:8-10 (NLT)*

Bring your cracks, your scars, your wounds to the Potter. He will bind them up. He will make you whole again. You won't be the same. You will be uniquely you; exquisitely beautiful. He will use you to reach others who need hope in their brokenness. Oh, when the Potter's light shines through you, it will be a thing of beauty; it will reflect and bounce off the joined pieces, and that glorious light will draw others. When they come, tell them about the Potter. Broken vessels are especially valuable to Him.

Blue Broken Glass Treasure Takeaway:

Your broken pieces are especially precious to God. He is the glue that will bind them together. He will make you beautifully whole and useful again.

Optional:

Questions for Personal Growth or Small Group Discussion can be found on page 100.

chapter 6

BLUE EARPLUGS

Understand this, my dear brothers and sisters:
You must be <u>quick</u> to listen, and <u>slow</u> to speak.
James 1:19 (NLT)

There they were. The blue earplugs. As with the other blue things, they were right in front of me. I laughed when I saw them because God knows listening is an area I need to improve. (John, if you are reading this, I know you are nodding in agreement.) In my defense, it isn't all my fault, it's my brain's fault. It's constantly in a whirl, so I'm easily distracted. One minute I'm listening – the next, my thoughts shift to any number of things… groceries needed, a friend I haven't seen in a while… you get the idea. Now where was I? Ah, yes – the need to become a better listener. Agreed and Amen. After all, God gave us two ears and one mouth for a reason.

Slow to speak is another issue for me, but God didn't give me any of Sadie's blue duct tape on the road, so I believe He's paving the way for this to be a message on listening <u>only</u>. *Thank you, gentle Jesus.* Slow to speak… let's save that topic for another day. Listening – here we come.

There was an elderly man who struggled with hearing. His wife pleaded with him for many years to get hearing aids. Eventually he gave in and saw an audiologist. Upon returning home he shared the good news with his wife. "My dear," he said, "I finally got my ears checked and am now the proud owner of a new state-of-the art hearing device." "Wonderful news!" she exclaimed, then asked him – "what kind it is?" He responded, "2:30."

That's a joke. I borrowed it. One that I think speaks to the need to hear with clarity. It appears that the elderly man's new hearing device needed a little more fine-tuning.

Fine tuning. When I was eight years old, I had a pretty bad pneumonia and ended up in the hospital for a week. Back in the 70s, hospitals had more rules about visitors than they do today, and those rules were strictly enforced. Visitors could come late in the mornings and early in the evenings. No overnight companions sleeping in a chair next to you; not even your parents. As a kid, nighttime was a bit scary.

One evening, Dad stopped in after work with a little gift. It was a small red, white, and blue AM/FM transistor radio. The front had a big round dial, and the top had an antenna that I could extend. Best of all, it came with earphones so I could plug into the radio and listen to music without disturbing the kid I shared a room with. I think Dad got it for me to take away the sting of separation. It did help as it was a pleasant distraction – especially at night.

Turning the power on was easy but getting the music to come in clearly – not so easy. I'd roll my finger over the dial and hear a little bit of music with a lot of static sounds. The closer I got to the station, the clearer it came in, but go a little too far and out it went again. It usually took several tries before I'd dial in "just right" and the music would come through clearly.

Victory! With my favorite music playing, I'd lay back into the pillow, headphones on, and think I was pretty cool. After leaving the hospital, I continued to enjoy the radio and, over time, I got better at dialing into my favorite station. Practice makes perfect.

Dialing into the voice of God is kind of like that. It takes some effort, some time, but above all, it takes a relationship with Him. The more time we spend with Him, the more in-tune we will become. Take my Mom, for example.

Mom was sitting in the waiting area of her doctor's office. She was dressed in a nice velour jogging suit. A black one. You know the type – stretch waist pants with a matching jacket that zips up the front. Even though she's in her early 80s, she makes an effort to look nice whenever she goes out – regardless of where she's headed. So, there she was – all nice looking, when a younger woman sitting in a chair across from her complimented Mom. "Your outfit is real pretty," she said. Mom smiled and said, "Thank you." They proceeded to make some small talk. After a while they quieted down and took magazines to occupy their time.

As Mom flipped through the pages of hers, she heard a voice. That voice said, *Give her money to get a new jogging suit like yours.* There was only one other person in the waiting room, so she knew who the voice was directing her to. Mom glanced over at the young woman and noticed that she was wearing worn jeans and a sweatshirt fraying at the cuffs. Since it was an awkward request, Mom would need a little more coaxing and went back to reading.

Soon the voice returned. *Linda, give her money to get a new jogging suit.* Mom, knowing it was God's voice, silently spoke back and told Him she didn't have any cash with her. Back to the magazine she went. Yet again, the voice returned – with the same instruction. Wanting to be obedient, she leaned forward to the woman across from her and said, "Excuse me, but would you mind telling me your name?" The woman looked puzzled. Mom continued, "God wants to give you money for a new jogging suit, but I don't have cash. I'd like to write you a check, that's why I need your name." The check was written and passed to the woman. "Now," Mom added, "make sure you get a good one. I suggest you go over to Boscov's Department Store, that's where I got mine."

This story makes me smile. It's just so – Mom. When she believes God is asking her to do something, more often than not – she does. She truly is in-tune with hearing His voice. Maybe it's because she's been listening to Him for 80 some years.

Figure 9 Mom all dressed up

We are about to veer off course just a bit, so hang in there with me – there's a method to the madness. Let's explore a children's book by Dr. Seuss. Yes – Dr. Seuss. Are you familiar with *Horton Hears a Who?* It's a family favorite in the Williams household. John read that book over and over and over again to three of our youngest (Dominic, Sophie, and Rachel) when they were little. They begged him to read it, because he used funny voices for all the different characters. John read that book so many times he eventually could tell the entire story from memory. That's 1,626 words. Impressive!

Any "Who…"

Horton was an elephant. Elephants have big ears and so he had a gift for hearing things others could not. One day, Horton heard a tiny voice coming from a speck of dust. The voice was that of a Who, living in Who-Ville. There wasn't anyone in Horton's community that could hear the Who's voice except for Horton so they thought he was crazy. Ultimately, he needed to prove that the Who and all of Who-Ville existed. If he couldn't do so, Horton's community plotted to toss the speck of dust (the Who-Ville habitat) into a pot of boiling Beezele-Nut oil!

Horton, in an attempt to save their lives, pleaded with the residents of Who-Ville to gather together and combine their voices, hoping the sound would be loud enough for the non-believers to hear. They shouted from the top of their lungs, '*We are here, we are here, we are here. WE ARE HERE, WE ARE HERE, WE ARE HERE!!!*' Eventually, their voices were heard. Horton was vindicated and the Who people were narrowly saved.

As Mary Ethel Eckard would say, "Now that'll preach." What will preach is this. We need to be more like Horton and tune into the small voice and to who's behind the voice. Indeed, who IS behind the voice of God? God the Father, God the Son, and God the Holy Spirit! Three in one and, like the Who's in Who-Ville, they are begging to be heard.

Quiet yourself for just a minute… tune in… can you hear them whisper to your heart? *We are here… we are here… we are here. We Are Here, We Are Here, We Are Here. <u>WE</u> ARE HERE. <u>WE</u> ARE HERE. <u>WE</u> ARE HERE!!!* Whisper back to them. *I hear you. I am listening.*

I encourage you to take a moment and just sit in their glorious presence. Then, come back here and we will continue.

We are going to turn now to two stories from the Bible. One from the Old Testament (before Jesus entered the world) and a New Testament story using Jesus' own words.

First up to bat is the Old Testament story from 1 Kings, Chapter 19. It's the story of a man (a prophet) named Elijah. He was desperate to hear God's voice because he needed His help and guidance. Things had gotten so bad; he was literally running for his life. He eventually found a cave on Mount Sinai and hid there. That's where he was when he encountered God.

> *As Elijah stood there on the mountain, the LORD passed by, and a mighty windstorm hit the mountain. It was such a terrible blast that the rocks were torn loose, but the LORD was not in the wind. After the wind there was an earthquake, but the LORD was not in the earthquake. And after the earthquake there was a fire, but the LORD was not in the fire. And after the fire there was <u>the sound of a gentle whisper</u>. When Elijah heard it, he wrapped his face in his cloak and went out and stood at the entrance of the cave.*
> *1 Kings 19:11-13 (NLT)*

To look for God only in powerful, miraculous ways may be to miss Him, because He is often found gently whispering in the quietness of a humbled heart.

Quietness is key to tuning in. How do we decrease the noise around us in such a loud, demanding, chaotic world, with so many things begging for our attention? We have to make an effort. We need to find a quiet place to get away with God. It's not easy, but worth every precious minute. Maybe we need to silence our cell phones for a little while or go for a quiet walk. Maybe it's getting up a few minutes earlier in the morning and reading just one chapter in the Bible. Where there's a will there's a way.

Mary of Bethany found a way, and how she found it is written in the book of Luke, chapter 10. The backstory goes something like this. One of Jesus' best friends was Lazarus. Jesus loved him and his two sisters – Martha and Mary. So, when He was traveling through the area, He stopped by their home to visit. Martha got right to work making things nice for Jesus… cleaning, cooking… That's when she saw Mary. Mary wasn't doing a thing except sitting at Jesus' feet. It frustrated Martha so she complained to Jesus.

"Lord, doesn't it seem unfair to you that my sister just sits here while I do all the work? Tell her to come and help me." But the Lord said to her, "My dear Martha, you are worried and upset over all these details! There is only one thing worth being concerned about. Mary has discovered it, and it will not be taken away from her."
Luke 10:40-42 (NLT)

The way Mary discovered it was to quiet herself before the Lord; to sit at His feet and simply soak in His presence and His words. This seems so opposite of what the world tells us to do. *"Don't just sit there – do something."* Yet here, it seems that Jesus is saying, *"Don't just do something – sit with Me."* After soaking in the goodness of Jesus, I'm sure Mary helped her sister; but for a little while she chose a higher calling.

Both Mary and Elijah experienced God. They looked, they listened... they found. You and I can too.

In this chapter we had an opportunity to meet some interesting characters: Mom, Horton, Elijah and Mary. I find it encouraging that all found the right setting on their individual radios and their effort was worth it. Mom's fine tuning led to an act of obedience. Horton's fine tuning saved lives. Elijah's fine tuning led to God's guidance. Mary's fine tuning caused her to stop and sit in the presence of Jesus so she could focus on His words. I believe if you and I will tune-in, we will find it of great value as well. But don't take my word for it. Take God at His word.

> *Be still and know that I am God.*
> *Psalm 46:10 (NLT)*

What exactly is God asking of us when He says, "Be still"? Does He want us to quit moving around for a few minutes? Focus? Those are helpful things indeed, yet there's more. The Hebrew word translated as "be still" is râphâh, which literally means "to let go" or to "release." So maybe, just maybe – what He's asking of us is to let go of (even just briefly) whatever it is that takes up our head space, that we might fill it instead with Him: His Love, His wisdom, His guidance...His deep and abiding peace.

Blue Earplugs Treasure Takeaway:

Dial into God. A little fine tuning (quiet time) is a great way to begin. Let go, release. Receive.

Optional:

Questions for Personal Growth or Small Group Discussion can be found on page 102.

chapter 7

BLUE ODDS /
BLUE MOUNTAIN LAKE

Trust in the Lord with all your heart; do not
depend on your own understanding.
Seek His will in all you do, and He will direct your paths.
Proverbs 3:5-6 (NLT)

The next few chapters (7 thru 9) are things that I discovered AFTER God gave me the bag of blue stuff. Yet, I believe they are things He wants included in this book. Some blue odds and ends. And this particular chapter is definitely worthy of checking off the "odds" box. Here goes…

A wild goose chase was about to begin in the back yard. Annie, our black Lab, heard them squawking and ran to the edge of the pond. Above the treetops they came, flying in formation. They made a quick pass over the water, across the field, then disappeared briefly before making a magnificent splash landing. Annie was ready for action and jumped into the pond after them. She swam in their direction, but they quickly paddled away, honking loudly. I'm not sure if the honking was meant as a distress signal or simply a way to taunt an old dog. Regardless, after several attempts to reach them, she succumbed to defeat and climbed out of the water and sat in the tall grass watching them.

Figure 10 Annie waiting for the geese to land

Like Annie, I've been on a wild goose chase myself a time or two... maybe more, but who's counting. Want to join me on one of them?

John and I had a vacation planned for our family long before the blue stuff. Our destination? BLUE Mountain Lake in the Adirondacks. We were staying at an Adirondack great camp, "The Hedges," that dated back to the 1880's. John and I had been there before, but it was a first for our children, and we were all excited to be going. With a pristine lake, canoes and kayaks, and nearby trails, we had plenty of opportunities for adventure.

On day two of our vacation, we decided to go on a hike to Castle Rock – a moderate three-mile loop trail with a spectacular view of the lake and mountains. As we climbed our way toward the summit, we talked about the blue stuff I'd recently collected. We decided to treat the pieces like pieces of a puzzle. The kids eagerly added their thoughts as to what they might mean. They had some wonderful ideas, which led to interesting conversation. We never arrived at a conclusion – but it was great fun. After the hike we returned to our cabin in the woods.

That night, we sat in the camp's historic dining room. We were hungry from our morning's adventure. On our table I saw a note from the owner, Pat Benton. It was an invitation for all campers to attend a meeting (if they wanted to) about the future of The Hedges. Pat had owned the property for many years, but it was time to sell. She wanted to ensure that it would remain accessible to families for years to come so, rather than sell it to one private buyer, she decided it would be best to see if a coalition of past campers would come together to purchase it. Valued at over three million dollars, she definitely needed a number of serious campers committed to that sort of investment.

The meeting was scheduled for Sunday, our last day there. We weren't planning to attend. Participating in a multi-million-dollar purchase was definitely not in our financial plan. Not even close. The vacation itself was a splurge. Instead, we invested our money into a half day boat rental. We hopped on and off the pontoon, exploring little islands that dotted the lake. We ate bagged lunches on one of them. The kids and John did a little fishing as we drifted along. When suddenly… it came to me. My mind took me down a path that looked like this:

Oh my gosh – I think God gave me the blue stuff to draw my attention to BLUE things. Then He brought us to BLUE Mountain Lake, to this magnificent camp. A property that just happens to be for sale. AND there's a meeting that just happens to be in 30 minutes about the sale. AND I'm pretty sure He wants me to attend. My heart pounded. Could it be

that GOD WANTS TO GIVE ME THE HEDGES?!! He
knows I have a love for retreats. It would be just like Him to
provide a permanent home for the retreats so people can draw
nearer to Him in the quiet of nature.

I literally got myself so worked up at the possibilities, that I got "lift off"
(when you aren't grounded in reality). But three million dollars?!! I decided
that NOTHING WAS IMPOSSIBLE with God!!! He just needed to get
to work quickly to inform Pat of His plan too; because clearly – she hadn't
gotten the message yet.

Now, my husband has always been very supportive when it comes to my
passion to follow what I believe to be God's will. When I shared with John
that I felt God wanted me to offer a weekly Women's Bible Study in our
home, he was completely on board. When I sensed God leading me to
organize the Extreme Retreat scaling Mount Marcy, John didn't hesitate
to support it. When I turned our barn into a retreat facility for a day and
60 ladies attended, John helped in every way possible. Yet, when I shared
with him what I believed God wanted to do with the Hedges… John gave
me a "you might be a little off-track on this one" look. Nonetheless, he
agreed to take me to the dock and drop me off just in time for the meeting.

The meeting was about to begin. I didn't have time to run to the cabin to
clean up first. My hair was windblown from the boat ride, I was wearing
shorts and a t-shirt over my still damp swimsuit. On my feet I had crocs,
and in my hands, I carried a stack of wet towels that needed to be returned
to housekeeping before we left. When I walked into the meeting, I did
NOT look like an investor at all. Everyone else, mostly men, was dressed
in "business casual" attire – khaki slacks, button down shirts; a few even
had on sports jackets. I cringed at my appearance. What was I thinking?
I quickly sat at a table; eager to hide behind it.

Pat welcomed everyone to the meeting. She was just getting started when another thought came to me. Perhaps it would be helpful for her to know that I am a CHRISTIAN; how else would she know who to give The Hedges to when God informed her of His plan. So… just before she dove into the program, I raised my hand. She looked at me and said, "Yes?" I spoke. "Would it be ok if I opened us in prayer? I think it would be a lovely way to begin." The room was quiet. All eyes were on me – looking at me like I had three heads. The expression on Pat's face did NOT make me think a "yes" was forthcoming, but she acquiesced. The prayer was over, and no one seemed to be moved by my words. Pat went ahead with her program.

As I sat at the table and looked around, I realized this wasn't God's will at all, it was something I WANTED, and I was trying my best to manipulate the outcome. Clearly, it wasn't working. There wasn't going to be any land transfer planned in my favor; nor for the future retreaters that I thought would be coming. I felt like a fool. My treasure hunt with God took a wrong turn. All because I was listening to my own voice; not His. I got ahead of Him. I was trying to force pieces together that didn't fit.

Pat was only a few minutes into her meeting when I tried my best to nonchalantly slip out the side door; the stack of wet towels still in my hands. It was an embarrassing lesson, but one I can now laugh at. THY will; not <u>MY</u> will be done. It turned out to be a wild goose chase. A chase of my own doing.

An interesting tidbit – Did you know that Celtics used the wild goose as a symbol for the Holy Spirit instead of a dove? There's quite a contrast between the two – wouldn't you agree? When I think of the Holy Spirit as a dove, I envision a peaceful fluttering; a gentle whisper in the wind. When I think of a wild goose – anything but that. They are untamed and unpredictable. Yet I can see why the Celtics might have chosen that symbol when you consider the way the Spirit moves unpredictably in our lives.

> *The wind blows where it chooses, and you hear the sound*
> *of it, but you do not know where it comes from or where it*
> *goes. So it is with everyone who is born of the Spirit.*
> *John 3:8 (NCB)*

When I consider the Blue Mountain goose chase, it began with a thought – not an interior prompting from the Spirit of God. But that same Spirit that I got ahead of, got me back on track and settled down. The treasure hunt continued.

Blue Odds / Blue Mountain Lake Treasure Takeaway:

Don't get ahead of God's plan. To avoid "lift off," keep your eyes toward heaven and your feet grounded on earth. Remember, *Thy Will, not My Will, be done.*

Optional:

Questions for Personal Growth or Small Group Discussion can be found on page 104.

chapter 8

BLUE DRU / BLUE GLOVE

Pure and genuine religion in the sight of God the Father
means caring for orphans and widows in their distress
and refusing to let the world corrupt you.
James 1:27 (NLT)

Politics and religion are two topics that can draw us together or separate us. The 2020 presidential race is a prime example from a "separate us" perspective. Not only was the Nation divided, but families were divided. My extended family was no exception, so we decided (as a family) not to broach the subject at get-togethers. In the same way, religion can create fractures in families just as readily. I'm not about to dive into politics, but I am going to wade – just ankle deep – into the waters of religion to share a few thoughts.

I was raised a Catholic. My parents are Catholic and the generations that went before them were all Catholic. But through my own fault, poor decisions and sin, I fell away… not just from my Catholic faith – but from God. I was lost. My spiritual compass was broken. I wandered aimlessly, searching for something to stand on.

In my search, I attended several Baptist services. There I found a conviction to read Scripture, but it didn't feel like home. Next, I attended (for quite some time) services at an Episcopal church. There I discovered the joy of small group Bible studies. I met remarkable ladies who mentored me as my passion for God's Word grew, but it still didn't feel like home. Then one day, I returned to a Catholic church and everything about it was home to me.

I came to understand that, without knowing it, I was collecting pieces of these beautiful places of worship and carrying them with me. Pieces... like my love for the Bible, my passion for Small Group Studies and Women's Ministry. Those pieces I did not leave behind, rather I was able to carry them with me to my new church home. One of the things I discovered: Jesus is in all of those congregations, because He is present whenever two or more are gathered in His name. Let us not, therefore, stand in judgement of which religion is right or wrong. Rather, let's celebrate that Jesus is alive and well in all Christian faiths through His glorious resurrection and in His people.

I pray that my words are received in the manner with which they are written. One of pure love. That being said, let's move on to … *caring for orphans and widows in their distress.*

A few weeks had passed since the blue treasure hunt morning, yet the memory of it was still fresh. I found myself revisiting each piece God had given me. They were like little rocks tossed onto a beach by crashing waves, then pulled back into the ocean as the water retreats. Only to be tossed onto the shore again – always landing in a different spot. *What does all of this mean, if there's a meaning to any of it at all? Am I trying to make something of nothing? Am I trying to see you, God, in all of this when it really wasn't anything but trash along a roadside?*

I was desperate for some clarity. *Okay, God, let's go for one more morning walk. Same route. Same request. God if there is anything you want me to see that will help give me direction in my life, please put it on the road in front of me so I will know it's from you.* I guess what I was hoping for was another blue piece that would tie all the loose ends together.

I passed the half mile point and, so far, nothing was on the road in front of me. Soon the mile marker came and went. Two miles, yet there was still nothing to be found. Nothing blue. Nothing at all. I was about to say, *Well, God – guess I've just been on a wild goose chase,* when suddenly I heard, "Hello there!" coming from behind a tall bush next to the road. As I passed the bush, I saw a tiny woman leaning on the end of a snow shovel. She was wearing a long skirt and a *Little House on the Prairie* style sunbonnet to shade her face. She also just happened to be wearing a blue sweater. Seeing the sweater and the shade of blue, I began to think that perhaps this was another of God's blue things. Only this wasn't a blue thing – it was a blue someone and blue could hardly be used to describe her sunny disposition.

"Well, hello to you," I responded; then asked, "What are you shoveling?" "Leaves," she said. "I find them easier to move with a shovel when they are on the driveway. A rake is a little too challenging." She extended her hand to me and introduced herself. "My name is Druscilla, but you can call me Dru. Everyone calls me Dru." I took her hand and shook it. "Pleased to meet you Dru, I'm Patty. I live on the other side of that hill," pointing over my left shoulder.

Dru was close to 90 years old. Her bright blue eyes sparkled, giving away a hint of mischievousness and just a tad bit of stubbornness. I couldn't help but smile at her; she was so cute in the bonnet. I asked Dru if she'd mind if I took a whack at the leaf shoveling. She cheerfully agreed. After the last few leaves were bagged up and placed at the curb, I walked her to her door. She used her walker. Up the rickety wooden ramp she rolled. The walker had a fold down seat. Before entering her doorway, she stopped and placed a few sticks of firewood on the seat and off she rolled again toward her kitchen. I asked if I could help bring in more firewood, and once more she gratefully accepted the offer.

After several logs were stacked inside, Dru invited me to sit with her at the kitchen table. We had a lovely chat. She told me that she grew up in the farmhouse two doors down and the home she lived in now once belonged to her grandparents. This was an old house, a very old house indeed. The primary heat source was a massive cast iron stove (from the late 1800s) that was in the center of the kitchen. A wide stove pipe went up through the ceiling, into the second floor and out the rooftop. The stove generated heat to most of the rooms as well as upstairs.

The left side of the stove was where she put in the firewood. During the cold weather, she never let the flame go out. The right side was the oven. The top could easily accommodate up to six large pots or skillets. The logs she wanted stacked seemed dangerously close to the stove, but she assured me it wasn't a fire hazard. However, looking around, I'd say the entire house was a fire hazard. There were extension cords hung willy-nilly all around the room and strung through doorways into adjoining rooms. Yikes. No fire hazards here.

At her age and physical condition, I found it hard to envision Dru heating her home in such a challenging manner. Surely a relative or friend helped with the delivery and stacking of the wood. The more we spoke, the more I learned about my new friend. She adored her husband, Al, but he passed away a few years prior. Dru missed him immensely and confided that, for a while after he died, she gave up the will to live.

Her neighbor, Rick, saw that she became quite thin and, out of concern, began eating meals with her so she wouldn't be so lonely. Slowly she got back on her feet. Out of the three children Dru and Al had, only one was still alive and he lived in Nashville, Tennessee- almost a thousand miles away, and he had cancer. Rick, the neighbor (who was like a son), and his lovely wife, Marsha, lived across the street and they helped her as much as they could, yet they worked and weren't always available.

When Dru and I ended our morning chat, I continued on my way home. All I could think about was Dru and her blue sweater, when low and behold another blue item was on the road in front of me. A blue work glove with a thick rubberized blue palm. Now, maybe I'm just crazy or trying too hard to make something out of nothing, but I honestly sensed that God was saying *thank you for being my helping hand today*. When I arrived home, I went into my closet and pulled out the bag of blue stuff and added the glove to my collection.

Figure 11 Dru with me, Rachel and Sophie

That morning was not my only visit with Dru. We began to spend quite a bit of time together. I began to pop in regularly to check on her, always grabbing a load of firewood as I walked into her house. I'd occasionally bring over dinner or drive her to doctor appointments. John and the kids enjoyed her as well. They helped chop and stack firewood, shovel her driveway in the winter, and rake leaves in the fall. She enjoyed their visits very much. With Rick and Marsha across the road helping when they could, and the Williams family, plus one or two lady friends from Dru's church occasionally dropping by, Dru's situation had improved.

One day when we were driving home from a doctor's appointment, Dru asked if it would be ok to put me down as one of her healthcare proxy's. She said she wanted two proxies, and the other was Rick. At first it surprised me. I had only known her for a year. That seemed like a big "ask," but understanding she had no family close by, I could see the need for it. I agreed to take on that role.

Dru called me frequently, especially if something was needed from the grocery store – to save her the drive into town. But one day her need was different. She called because she had taken a fall in her house. I met the ambulance there. She wasn't seriously injured, but they took her to the hospital to be sure. She hadn't been feeling well leading up to the fall. While at the hospital, they discovered she had advanced cancer; her health was failing rapidly. Per her wishes, surgery was performed to remove a large mass, but it took a toll on her. A week later, Rick and I were consulted to make some very hard decisions for Dru because she wasn't coherent. Decisions we never wanted to make, but we had no option, as her surgeon informed us that she wouldn't recover.

On the morning of July 19, 2017, when I arrived at the hospital, Dru was alone. I stood beside her and held her tiny, bruised hand. All tubes had been removed from her and she was well into the dying process. She was unconscious. Her breathing slow. Then a long pause followed by a brief rattled breath. I climbed into bed next to her and cradled her in my arms. I prayed The Lord's Prayer aloud and sang a hymn that was meaningful to her. Five minutes later… she was gone. They say that someone might wait to pass until they are alone or choose to hang in there until someone is with them. Dru must have wanted the latter. It gave me comfort that she didn't die alone. I believe God didn't want her to be alone either.

My precious little Dru, her blue sweater and sparkling blue eyes peering from beneath the bonnet – that is how I will forever remember her. I thanked God that He gave me the opportunity to be one of His helping hands in her final two years on Earth. I thanked God for the little army of helpers He assembled, too. I thanked God that He blessed me with a chance to walk with her to the threshold of death – knowing Jesus would walk with her the rest of the way. It was an honor to have shared, ever so briefly, in her life's journey, and I am far richer for having known her. She was, and always will be, a treasure in my life.

Dru's son from Tennessee arranged to have her cremated. I believe it was Rick who collected Dru's ashes from the funeral home and took them to the old farmhouse she had lived in. A few weeks later, one of Dru's friends planned a small celebration of life at their church. I was asked to speak about Dru. Once again, I thought it odd that someone who knew her so briefly would be asked to do this, but it was an honor, as I so adored her. Before going, I sat down to write some thoughts… wondering what to say. When the words came so fast, I knew God was giving them to me. All I had to do was put them on paper.

In essence, this is what came to me. I felt that if Dru could speak for herself, it would be a message of being thankful. Nearly every time one of us did something for her, she'd say the following: "THANK YOU is just eight little letters, but they come from a heart FULL of gratitude." So, on her behalf, I used the opportunity to be her voice and, by name, I thanked all I could think of who had touched Dru's life.

About a year after Dru surrendered her spirit to God, her old farmhouse surrendered to the forces of nature. A fire leveled the entire structure, likely caused by bad wiring – no surprise there! Later, I discovered that Dru and Al's ashes were still inside. There is beauty in that, don't you think? Their earthly bodies returned to the soil on property they dearly loved; while their spirits now dance together in the radiant light of God.

And so, my dear friends – if God brings a Dru into your life, know that you are being entrusted with one of His greatest treasures. Slip on that blue glove and offer a helping hand. The blessing will be yours.

Let your roots grow down into Him, and let your lives be built on Him. Then your faith will grow strong in the truth you were taught, and you will overflow with THANKFULNESS.
Colossians 2:7 (NLT)

Blue Dru / Blue Glove Treasure Takeaway:

Have a thankful heart. And be aware of those God brings into your life –
they may need a helping hand.

Optional:

Questions for Personal Growth or Small Group Discussion can be found
on page 106.

chapter 9

BLUE COAT

Now if you will obey me and keep my covenant,
you will be my own special treasure from among all the peoples on earth;
for all the earth belongs to me.
Exodus 19:5(NLT)

My dad worked hard to provide for our very large family. He had a blue-collar job; over-worked and underpaid – at least from my family's perspective. Yet as a child, my parents never shared with me or my siblings just how tight finances were. We never went without our basic needs being met.

Mom was good at stretching the budget. She found ways to skimp and save. Instead of milk in a carton, there was Carnation Instant Milk. Instead of ground beef; we had venison (my dad was an avid hunter – as much for food on the table as it was for sport). Mom found discounted clothing for us, or we were given hand-me-downs by family friends. The love in our family made up for whatever else might have been lacking. We were happy.

My parents had five children in six years (no twins – individual births), a typical Catholic family in the 60s. Several years later (1976) my baby sister, Amy, was born. An oops baby? No such thing! She was OUR baby and we, much older siblings, ADORED her!

Mom's parents moved to Florida around the time Amy was born and it was heartbreaking for her. Mom was very close to Nana and Pop. When Amy was just a toddler, Mom decided to visit them. The whole family wasn't going, just Mom and Amy. Family finances, school for us older kids – these were the things that they took into consideration when making that decision. Mom booked a ticket on a Greyhound bus. It was the least expensive way to travel there. Airfare wasn't an option.

Can you imagine traveling to Florida from New York by bus, with a toddler? I can't. It was a long, hard trip with stop after small-town-stop. Bus station after bus station, picking up more passengers and some getting off. Public rest rooms with a toddler in tow. Mom was weary and a little angry with God that she had to travel in this manner. She didn't hold back when she spoke with Him (in prayer). *Why, God, must we have so little? It seems so unfair that some people have the ability to hop on an airplane and here we are – on a bus.* She barely got the words out of her mouth when God stopped her in her tracks. *"Because," He said, "instead of wealth – I have given you my jewels, my treasure... your children."* Her discontent vanished and was immediately replaced with a heart full of gratitude. Her children... her treasure; HIS treasure. She wouldn't trade her children for all the money in the world.

Figure 12 Mom's treasure multiplied
Her jewels – 6 children and their spouses, 17 grandchildren & 4 great grandchildren

So, what does the Greyhound bus story have to do with a blue coat? Well, I'm glad you asked...

Eight years after the treasure hunt unfolded, I was hiking at a local state park. It was a chilly day in late autumn. Leaves were scattered among the path and crunched beneath my feet. The sky was gray; a reflection of my spirit – which was heavy once again. That nagging feeling returned, the one that visited me often when my world was quiet. The blue stuff... my treasure hunt with God stuff that was initially so much fun. Ugh! *Where's the fun now, Lord?* The pieces had become a weight around my neck, and I couldn't free myself of them. They haunted me. I was so tired of having those same thoughts return over and over again. Jeremiah's words came to me once more... *His Word was in my heart like a burning fire shut up in my bones; I was weary of holding it back, and I could not.*

Weary. *I am weary God. What will it take for me to finally have peace? When will my Spirit rest within me? Will I be taunted forever until I step out of the boat – like Peter did? How will I know you will be there to keep me from sinking into deep water? Do I press you for one last sign that this is Your will and not mine?*

And I did.

God, would you give me one last blue thing, so I know YOU are behind this madness?!

I walked along the wooded path. Deeper and deeper into the forest. It was a path I'd never been on. Not a single blue thing anywhere. Nothing blue on the path directly in front of me. Nothing blue to my left or to my right – yes, I looked there too. Even though I committed to God I wouldn't do that on our first walk together in 2015. Do you see how desperate I was? In an effort to get peace on the matter, I was taking matters into my own hands. Going off the beaten path instead of keeping my eyes ahead and on Him. Naturally He wasn't going to let me find a blue thing where He hadn't led me to look.

Onward I went. The walk was nearly completed, and I came up empty handed. Nothing blue – except my disposition. *Nothing blue except me.* Those thoughts resonated in my Spirit. Then a word from God. *Did you notice you are wearing a blue coat? It took you a while, but glad you finally caught on. YOU are my treasure and I love you with an everlasting love!*

Oh, the infinite love of our God!!! He melted my heart. My friend, you who have been on this treasure hunt with me, do you know that you are God's treasure too? I am NOT His favorite child, YOU are! We all are!!! Do you know how deeply He loves you – uniquely you, completely you?

His love is the foundation on which all things are built. Nothing makes sense in our lives until we fully embrace HIS LOVE.

> He whispers "I love you" in the stillness of our hearts.
> He writes it across the sky in the magnificence of His creation.
> He will physically touch us with His love through those He places in our lives.
> He even documented that love through the Bible so we wouldn't forget.

But most importantly,

> He sacrificed His only Son, Jesus, so we would never be separated from His love.
> Our world has never known such love and will never know one greater.

If you have ever struggled in receiving this great love, now is the time to settle the matter once and for all. I would like to share with you something I came across. Each statement in the letter that follows can be found in the Bible. Each statement is an unbreakable promise from your Heavenly Father.

I pray that He will soften your heart, even now, to prepare you for what you are about to read. I pray your indwelling Spirit of the Living God will jump with joy; and cover you with Holy Spirit goosebumps so you know and feel His presence. Amen.

Father's Love Letter – A Message from God to <u>You</u>
(Included with permission © 1999 Father Heart
Communications - FathersLoveLetter.com)

My Child,

You may not know me, but I know everything about you. I know when you sit down and when you rise up. I am familiar with all your ways. Even the very hairs on your head are numbered. For you were made in my image.

In me you live and move and have your being. For you are my offspring. I knew you even before you were conceived. I chose you when I planned creation. You were not a mistake, for all your days are written in my book. I determined the exact time for your birth and where you would live. You are fearfully and wonderfully made. I knit you together in your mother's womb. And brought you forth on the day you were born.

I have been misrepresented by those who don't know me. I am not distant and angry, but am the complete expression of love. And it is my desire to lavish my love on you. Simply because you are my child, and I am your Father. I offer you more than your earthly father ever could. For I am the perfect father.

Every good gift that you receive comes from my hand. For I am your provider and I meet all your needs. My plans for your future have always been filled with hope. Because I love you with an everlasting love. My thoughts toward you are countless as the sand on the seashore. And I rejoice over you with singing.

I will never stop doing good to you. For <u>you are my treasured possession</u>. I desire to establish you with all my heart and all my soul. And I want to show you great and marvelous things. If you seek me with all your heart, you will find me. Delight in me and I will give you the desires of your heart. For it is I who gave you those desires.

I am able to do more for you than you could possibly imagine. For I am your greatest encourager. I am also the Father who comforts you in all your troubles. When you are brokenhearted, I am close to you. As a shepherd carries a lamb, I have carried you close to my heart. One day I will wipe away every tear from your eyes. I will take away all the pain you have suffered on this earth.

I am your Father, and I love you even as I love my son, Jesus. For in Jesus, my love for you is revealed. He is the exact representation of my being. He came to demonstrate that I am for you, not against you. And to tell you that I am not counting your sins.

Jesus died so that you and I could be reconciled. His death was the ultimate expression of my love for you. I gave up everything I loved that I might gain your love. If you receive the gift of my son Jesus, you receive me. And nothing will ever separate you from my love again.

Come home and I'll throw the biggest party heaven has ever seen. I have always been Father, and will always be Father. My question is... Will you be my child? I am waiting for you.

Love,
Your Dad
Almighty God

The following is this letter broken down, verse by verse, and the location of each verse in the Bible. If a particular statement stood out to you, or caused you to pause, please take a few minutes to sit with that verse. Ask God to speak with you about it. Open the Bible and read the verse in context (maybe the whole chapter). Pray. Seek God's wisdom and His heart. He longs to commune with you.

You may not know me, but I know everything about you.	Psalm 139:1
I know when you sit down and when you rise up.	Psalm 139:2
I am familiar with all your ways.	Psalm 139:3
Even the very hairs on your head are numbered.	Matthew 10:29-31
For you were made in my image.	Genesis 1:27
In me you live and move and have your being.	Acts 17:28
For you are my offspring.	Acts 17:28
I knew you even before you were conceived.	Jeremiah 1:4-5
I chose you when I planned creation.	Ephesians 1:11-12
You were not a mistake, for all your days are written in my book.	Psalm 139:15-16
I determined the exact time for your birth and where you would live.	Acts 17:26
You are fearfully and wonderfully made.	Psalm 139:14
I knit you together in your mother's womb.	Psalm 139:13
And brought you forth on the day you were born.	Psalm 71:6
I have been misrepresented by those who don't know me.	John 8:41-44
I am not distant and angry, but am the complete expression of love.	1 John 4:16
And it is my desire to lavish my love on you.	1 John 3:1
Simply because you are my child, and I am your Father.	1 John 3:1
I offer you more than your earthly father ever could.	Matthew 7:11
For I am the perfect father.	Matthew 5:48
Every good gift that you receive comes from my hand.	James 1:17
For I am your provider and I meet all your needs.	Matthew 6:31-33
My plans for your future have always been filled with hope.	Jeremiah 29:11

Because I love you with an everlasting love.	Jeremiah 31:3
My thoughts toward you are countless as the sand on the seashore.	Psalm 139:17-18
And I rejoice over you with singing.	Zephaniah 3:17
I will never stop doing good to you.	Jeremiah 32:40
For you are my treasured possession.	Exodus 19:5
I desire to establish you with all my heart and all my soul.	Jeremiah 32:41
And I want to show you great and marvelous things.	Jeremiah 33:3
If you seek me with all your heart, you will find me.	Deuteronomy 4:29
Delight in me and I will give you the desires of your heart.	Psalm 37:4
For it is I who gave you those desires.	Philippians 2:13
I am able to do more for you than you could possibly imagine.	Ephesians 3:20
For I am your greatest encourager.	2 Thessalonians 2:16-17
I am also the Father who comforts you in all your troubles.	2 Corinthians 1:3-4
When you are brokenhearted, I am close to you.	Psalm 34:18
As a shepherd carries a lamb, I have carried you close to my heart.	Isaiah 40:11
One day I will wipe away every tear from your eyes.	Revelation 21:3-4
And I'll take away all the pain you have suffered on this earth.	Revelation 21:3-4
I am your Father, and I love you even as I love my son, Jesus.	John 17:23
For in Jesus, my love for you is revealed.	John 17:26
He is the exact representation of my being.	Hebrews 1:3
He came to demonstrate that I am for you, not against you.	Romans 8:31
And to tell you that I am not counting your sins.	2 Corinthians 5:18-19
Jesus died so that you and I could be reconciled.	2 Corinthians 5:18-19
His death was the ultimate expression of my love for you.	1 John 4:10
I gave up everything I loved that I might gain your love.	Romans 8:31-32
If you receive the gift of my son Jesus, you receive me.	1 John 2:23
And nothing will ever separate you from my love again.	Romans 8:38-39
Come home and I'll throw the biggest party heaven has ever seen.	Luke 15:7

I have always been Father, and will always be Father.	Ephesians 3:14-15
My question is... Will you be my child?	John 1:12-13
I am waiting for you.	Luke 15:11-32

Never doubt how deeply you are loved by Father God. YOU are His treasure! Do you treasure Him in response to that great love? Imagine all the love, all the power, all the glory He possesses is living in you. With each breath you take – He is there.

> *We now have this light shining in our hearts, but we ourselves are like fragile clay jars containing this great treasure. This makes it clear that our great power is from God, not from ourselves.*
> *2 Corinthians 4:7 (NLT)*

Blue Coat Treasure Takeaway:

YOU are God's treasure. You are loved. That is the foundation all else is built upon. Stand firmly on that foundation and step out in faith knowing He will be with you always – until the end of time.

Optional:

Questions for Personal Growth or Small Group Discussion can be found on page 108.

chapter 10

BLUE ENDS

I am the Alpha and the Omega, the First and
the Last, the Beginning and the End.
Revelation 22:13 (NLT)

The beginning and the end… how about a visual of that. If I asked you to get a piece of paper and a pencil and draw a circle, your starting and ending point would be the same, yet even after lifting the pencil from the paper, that line would never end. It goes on for infinity, and so it is with God. He is never ending, never changing. He is, and was, and always will be.

As we near the end of this little book and my pencil lifts from the paper one last time, there is one thing left to do. Let's take a brief look back to the beginning of this story to reflect on the jewels we've gathered along the way. Remember how it started?

> *God, I'm so tired. I want to please you, but this isn't working.*
> *I'm completely exhausted.* (THIS IS **SURRENDER**.)

> *Help me, Lord. I want to do your will, but I need clarity.*
> *I need your guidance in my life.* (THIS IS **PRAYER**.)

When Mary asked you for a dragonfly – You gave it to her. So, if You love me too, would You give me something all of my own? I'm humbly asking for a sign that will give me some direction. I'm not going to look to the left or to the right, I'm going to look directly on the road I'm traveling along – that way I'll know it's from You. (THIS IS **FAITH / FLEECE**.)

Father, I long to serve You and to be present to my family, with a renewed Spirit, so I trust You will work this out. Amen. (THIS IS **TRUST**.)

Now – let's dig in a little deeper:

SURRENDER is a moment in time when we realize that we cannot improve our situation in our own power. It's letting go of whatever we're holding onto in clenched fists, then opening our hands and placing that situation into God's hands.

1 Peter 5:6-7 says, *'Humble yourselves under the mighty power of God, and at the right time He will lift you up in honor. Give all your worries and cares to God, for He cares about you.'*

He cares about YOU! If that isn't enough reason to surrender, then hear this as well… His power works best in our weakness. Jesus is standing by, ready and willing to take that burden off our shoulders if we will just let Him. His yoke is easy, and His burden is light.

PRAYER is a two-way conversation with our Creator in which we not only speak with God, but we listen to Him. As His children, He longs to hear from us – in good times and bad. He also desires to be heard. He said,

"I will rescue those who love me. I will protect those who trust in my name. <u>When they call on me, I will answer;</u> I will be with them in trouble. I will rescue and honor them. I will reward them with a long life and give them my salvation."
Psalm 91:14-16 (NLT)

Speak with God about your circumstance and listen for His voice of wisdom.

FAITH is complete confidence is God. Believing without seeing. **FLEECE** is asking God for a sign. When Gideon needed God's guidance he asked for a sign.

"God, if you are truly going to use me to rescue Israel as you promised, prove it to me in this way. I will put a wool fleece on the threshing floor tonight. If the fleece is wet with dew in the morning but the ground is dry, then I will know you are going to help me rescue Israel as you promised. And that is just what happened. When Gideon got up early the next morning, he squeezed the fleece and wrung out a whole bowlful of water."
Judges 6:36-38 (NLT)

This was written before Jesus entered the world; before the Holy Spirit was given to us. With Jesus and the Holy Spirit, we shouldn't need to place a fleece before God. Yet, sometimes, He will respond to those fleece prayers (as He did with me). Maybe it's to jumpstart faith or to give us confidence to move in a direction. I guess He knew I needed a jumpstart that morning.

That being said, it's best to avoid the fleece and just go with faith – leaning into the wisdom and help provided by the Holy Spirit and the teachings of Jesus in Scripture. Faith shows spiritual maturity. Clearly, I need to develop my faith and give up the fleece.

When you have **SURRENDERED** your cares to God, and in **PRAYER** sought His help and guidance, and backed that up with **FAITH,** there's only one thing left to do. **TRUST** Him for the outcome.

What does trust look like? There's a quote by Franklin D. Roosevelt that I think illustrates this for us. *"When you reach the end of your rope, tie a knot in it and hang on."*

Trust is hanging onto God's promises while we wait for His response to our prayers. It might be a yes, a no, or a not-yet; but He always responds in His way and in His timing.

> *Jesus said, "If you trust me, you are trusting not only me, but also God who sent me. For when you see me, you are seeing the one who sent me. I have come as a light to shine in this dark world, so that all who put their trust in me will no longer remain in the dark."*
> *John 12:44-46 (NLT)*

Trust makes darkness disappear; so, put on trust and a pair of sunglasses, too.

The beginning… Alpha in Hebrew is *aleph* (the first letter in the Hebrew alphabet). The end… Omega in Hebrew is *tav* (the last letter in the Hebrew alphabet). Just now, this very moment, I did an on-line search for *tav*. I wanted to see if there was anything more behind this word. And guess what? There is. Here is what I discovered…

The Hebrew letter 'tav' symbolizes doing things with a goal in mind. We can compare it to a mountain climber who reaches the peak and accomplishes their goal.

Figure 13 Reaching the Summit

Woo-hoo! In that simple statement I feel indescribable joy. We, fellow treasure hunters, have reached the summit; "bagged our peak." *Peak bagging* is an expression avid hikers use to describe the act of climbing to the summit of a mountain, often to reach the highest point in a particular region. That's where I believe God is leading us now... to the grand summit to survey the landscape we've traveled together. In doing so, let's unpack our bag of blue, laying out all the pieces of treasure we've gathered along the way.

1. **BLUE FLIP FLOP:** Don't miss out on the dash – your personal encounter with the risen Lord. Confession is a gift that leads to peace. A clear conscience makes a soft pillow.

2. **BLUE SPOON:** Use the soft-spoon approach. Help others know God through your life; use words only when needed. And, above all – if you hear a gentle knock on your door, be sure to open it.

3. **BLUE LIGHTER:** God hears our prayers. He is our ever-present light in the darkness.

4. **BLUE PEN:** God speaks to us through the Bible. He loves you – uniquely you.

5. **BLUE BROKEN GLASS:** Your broken pieces are especially precious to God. He is the glue that will bind them together. He will make you beautifully whole and useful again.

6. **BLUE EARPLUGS:** Dial into God. A little fine tuning (quiet time) is a great way to begin. Let go, release. Receive.

7. **BLUE ODDS / BLUE MOUNTAIN LAKE:** Don't get ahead of God's plan. To avoid "lift off," keep your eyes toward heaven and your feet grounded on earth. Remember, *Thy Will, not my will, be done.*

8. **BLUE DRU / BLUE GLOVE:** Have a thankful heart. And be aware of those God brings into your life – they may need a helping hand.

9. **BLUE COAT:** YOU are God's treasure. You are loved. This is the foundation all else is built upon. Stand firmly on that foundation and step out in faith, knowing He will be with you always – until the end of time.

I love that there are 9 pieces that we pulled out of the bag because it was nine years ago when this treasure hunt started. And (this is so amazing) in biblical numerology, the number 9 symbolizes divine completeness or finality. Now that, my friends, is a God-fingerprint.

But what of my prayer to God so many years ago? I asked Him for clarity and guidance in my life. Did He ever answer my plea for help? He 100% did!

Seeking answers to my questions led me to spending more time (a lot more time) with Him. My relationship with God grew as He showed me the depth of His love for me and for all of humanity. He renewed my love of writing and gave me this book. I had to get out of the boat and trust Him, but He never let me down.

And so... I stand on this mountain top with a view of the valley below. I can see bits and pieces of the long, twisting path through breaks in the canopies of the trees. Some of the terrain was easy; other places it was so very hard. Times when I needed to climb over boulders, digging my toes and fingers into rock and soil just to pull myself up. Yet here I stand now with a glorious view of where I've been. It's all been worth it. The good, the bad... all of it a part of my past, leading me to the present. I wouldn't give up any of it knowing it drew me closer to our Living God.

I pray that your relationship with our Living God (God the Father, God the Son, and God the Holy Spirit) grows and grows.

And I am certain that God, who began a good work
within you, will continue His work until it is finally
finished on the day when Christ Jesus returns.
Philippians 1:6 (NLT)

Thank you for traveling with me... until we meet again...

<u>Optional:</u>

Questions for Personal Growth or Small Group Discussion can be found on page 110.

A BLESSING BEFORE YOU GO

Then the Lord said to Moses, "Tell Aaron and his sons to bless the people of Israel with this special blessing: May the Lord bless you and protect you. May the Lord smile on you and be gracious to you. May the Lord show you his favor and give you his peace." Whenever Aaron and his sons bless the people of Israel in my name, I myself will bless them.
Revelation 22:13 (NLT)

I almost forgot... the blessing. We can't end without a blessing! Mom never says good-bye without making a sign of the cross on our foreheads and saying, "Peace of Christ." That is her blessing for us. And, when I say "us," I mean all of her family, friends, even people she barely knows. She will bless anyone she can get her hands on. Literally.

I'd like to share her blessing with you now, with a sign of the cross on your forehead. *In the name of the Father, the Son, and the Holy Spirit. Peace of Christ to you, my friend! Amen.*

Figure 14 Mom blessing John at our wedding

Don't worry about anything; instead, pray about everything. Tell God what you need, and thank him for all he has done. Then you will experience God's peace, which exceeds anything we can understand. His peace will guard your hearts and minds as you live in Christ Jesus. And now, dear brother and sisters, one final thing. Fix your thoughts on what is true, and honorable, and right, and pure, and lovely, and admirable. Think about things that are excellent and worthy of praise. Keep putting into practice all you learned – then the God of peace will be with you.

QUESTIONS FOR PERSONAL GROWTH OR SMALL GROUP DISCUSSION

INTRODUCTION:

Read: Jeremiah 29:11-15

1. Of those five verses, which one resonates with you most and why?

2. Mary needed to know that God really loved her and asked Him for evidence of that love. In what ways has God shown you (in a tangible way) that you are uniquely loved by Him?

3. God gave Mary wings; their relationship grew exponentially after her dragonfly experience with Him. How would you describe your current relationship with God? Close? Stagnant? Distant? Explain.

4. Patty described a season in her life when she felt overwhelmed; biting off more than she could chew. Sometimes we add things to our plate that God didn't tell us to add. What are some ways you can avoid that pitfall?

5. Patty described feeling "hounded by God," to write about the blue things. Have you ever felt "hounded" by God for a specific task? Describe His request of you and how you responded.

6. What did you learn about God or yourself through the Introduction of this book?

CHAPTER 1 / BLUE FLIP-FLOP:

Read James 5:13-16

1. The earnest prayer of a _____ person has great power. (James 5:16) Why do you suppose this type of person's prayers are fruitful?

2. God doesn't care about our footwear, but He does care about how we live our lives. Do you believe you are glorifying God through your life? If yes, in what ways? If no, identify just one thing you could improve.

3. Saul went from persecuting Christians to becoming a Christian faith hero because of his dash encounter with Christ. Have you had a dash encounter? If so, what happened?

4. Jesus HAD to go to Samaria because there was a woman He had a divine appointment with. Their story gives us insight into His profound love for each of us. What was the result of that encounter?

5. *Contrite* is feeling or expressing remorse or penitence; affected by guilt. When was the last time you did some deep cleaning of your soul? If it's been a long time, what is keeping you from making a good confession? A clear conscience makes a soft pillow.

6. What did you learn about God or yourself through this chapter?

CHAPTER 2 / BLUE SPOON:

Read: Proverbs 15:4

1. What is a gentle word like? Why would it be described as such?

2. Have you ever made an attempt to share your faith with someone? If so, describe what happened.

3. Our job is to help plant seeds of faith. God's job is to grow those seeds. Have you ever tried to take on the "Grower's" job, trying to force the seeds to grow in your timing instead of His? What were the results?

4. Saint Teresa of Calcutta said, "Spread the love of God through your life, but only use words when necessary." Our actions speak louder than our words. Do your actions demonstrate God's love, if so – in what way?

5. Jesus knocks gently at our heart's door. He waits patiently for us to open it. How have you experienced the tender, gentle love of Jesus?

6. What did you learn about God or yourself through this chapter?

CHAPTER 3 / BLUE LIGHTER:

Read Matthew 12:18-21

1. Can you relate to the blue lighter on the road? Fallen to the wayside (a smoldering wick), but wanting to be useful again? There was still a spark in the old lighter. There is a spark in you too. What is needed for that little spark to become a flame?

2. Patty was having difficulty discerning if the *Extreme Retreat* was her idea or if the idea was from God. When you have struggled with discernment on a spiritual matter, how did you gain clarity?

3. Man plans and God laughs. What have you planned and tried to orchestrate without God's guidance and what were the results?

4. When we are at our lowest, Satan is often in our ear telling us how we have failed. He wants to separate us from God. How can you silence that voice?

5. The *phone call from God* became a "faith stone" for Patty. An experience with Him that she will carry throughout her life; something firm to stand on when difficult times come again. Do you have a faith stone? What do you stand on when the sand is shifting under your feet?

6. What did you learn about God or yourself through this chapter?

CHAPTER 4 / BLUE PEN:

Read John 1:1-5

1. The Bible is the Word of God, and the WORD is also Jesus. What additional things do we learn about the *WORD* from the verses we just read?

2. Imagine someone asked you to drive from your home to a particular address in Florida, but you couldn't use your GPS or MapQuest, not even a regular old paper map. You would probably make several wrong turns and a whole lot of gas station stops asking for directions. That's kind of what it's like to go through life without reading the Bible. How does the Bible give us guidance as we journey through life?

3. Doubting Thomas had a crisis in belief. He hit a high-speed-wobble, so Jesus gave him a hands-on experience. How can Jesus help us when we are faltering in faith? Read Mark 9:17-24. What is the father's prayer? (If you are struggling with faith, make that your prayer too. Jesus will respond and strengthen your faith.)

4. The Bible is one of the ways God speaks with us. If we aren't reading Scripture, then we are blocking an important avenue to hearing His voice. What small adjustment can you make so you can open the Living Word of God more frequently?

5. Patty described an encounter with God through Scripture. He *comforted* her through His Word, He counseled her on her situation, and gave her a life-verse. How would you describe the term 'life verse?' Is there a verse that is deeply meaningful to you? If so, what is it and why is it so important to you?

6. What did you learn about God or yourself through this chapter?

CHAPTER 5 / BLUE BROKEN GLASS:

Read 1 Peter 1:3-7

1. We sometimes suffer trials in our lives. What can result from these trials (verse 7)?

2. Patty brought pieces of broken glass to Michelle for the craft project. In what ways do we carry our broken pieces (from life experiences) into another person's life?

3. The Potter, our Heavenly Father, doesn't throw away the marred clay, instead He reshapes it according to His will. Clearly, the clay is valuable to Him even before it is transformed. Why do you think this is so?

4. After being reshaped, the clay is put into a furnace. The intense heat makes it strong. Does this resonate with you? If so, in what way?

5. Broken vessels are especially valuable to God. Why do you suppose that is?

6. What did you learn about God or yourself through this chapter?

CHAPTER 6 / BLUE EARPLUGS:

Read John 5:24-27

1. Jesus said, *Anyone who hears my words and believes in the one who sent me has eternal life and will not come to condemnation, but HAS ALREADY passed from* _____ *to* _____. (Fill in the blanks.) Explain the difference between *hearing* and *believing*; and why isn't *hearing* Jesus' words enough to pave the way for eternal life?

2. Are your spiritual ears open? If not, what steps do you need to take to improve your listening skills? Why is it so important to be a good listener?

3. When God makes a request of you, are you typically obedient? Or, do you try to hide from Him hoping He will find someone else for the job? If you are on the fence, what helps you to decide to help or hide?

4. Elijah needed God's protection and guidance. He was looking for Him in powerful, miraculous ways, yet ultimately found Him in a gentle whisper. Share something that you believe God has whispered to you.

5. *Be still and know that I am God.* Be still – release; let go. If you are clinging to something with your fingers closed tightly around it, there is no room in your hands to receive what God wants to put in them. What are you clinging to, that you believe God is asking you release into His care?

6. What did you learn about God or yourself through this chapter?

CHAPTER 7 / BLUE ODDS – BLUE MOUNTAIN LAKE:

Read Proverbs 3:5-6

1. When Patty set off on her *wild goose chase*, she was leaning on her own understanding. What would have happened if she had leaned on God's understanding instead? Verse 6 says, *In all your ways be mindful of Him and* _____ (fill in the blank). Do you tend to wait patiently for God's guidance, or rush ahead and hope He will bless your efforts?

2. Have you been on a wild goose chase of your own? Describe a time when you got ahead of God?

3. How can you prevent *lift-off*, to ensure you are staying within God's will?

4. Do you tend to view the Holy Spirit as a calm, fluttering dove of peace or as an unpredictable wild goose? Explain.

5. Does the verse, *"Thy will, not my will, be done"* bring you comfort or make you feel uncomfortable and why?

6. What did you learn about God or yourself through this chapter?

CHAPTER 8 / BLUE DRU – BLUE GLOVE:

Read Zechariah 7:9-10

1. What does the Lord ask us TO DO? What does He ask us NOT TO DO? Make a list for each below.

2. A Pharisee asked Jesus which commandment in the law is the greatest. How did Jesus respond? (Read Matthew 22:34-40). If we follow those commandments, the prior TO DO and NOT TO DO lists wouldn't be needed. TRUE or FALSE? _____ Explain your response.

3. Have you ever had anyone confront you about your religious beliefs? If so, what happened. What did you learn from that experience?

4. God placed people in Dru's life to help her. She was open to receiving help and, because of this, each person experienced joy that comes from serving others. When someone offers to help you: do you gratefully accept assistance; are you too embarrassed to accept help, or do you have an "I can do it myself" attitude? If you find it hard to accept a helping hand, what do you suppose is behind that?

5. Dru was always thankful. We sometimes are so focused on what we don't have that we lose sight of what we do have. How can we become more thankful for the good things God has given us?

6. What did you learn about God or yourself through this chapter?

CHAPTER 9 / BLUE COAT:

Read Matthew 6:19-21

1. *For where your treasure is, there your heart will be also.* In what ways have you been storing up earthly treasure? God wants us to store up treasures in heaven. What do you believe that means? Where is your heart today?

2. Patty's mom spoke to God and shared her frustrations with Him. In return, He helped her see things from a different perspective. Can you think of a time when God helped you see things through His eyes that changed your perspective on a situation?

3. Think of someone you treasure. What do you treasure about that person?

4. Do you find it hard to believe that you are God's treasure? Explain.

5. After reading *A Father's Love Letter*, which statement was most meaningful to you and why?

6. What did you learn about God or yourself through this chapter?

CHAPTER 10 / BLUE ENDS:

Read Isaiah 56:1-8

1. Where is God going to bring us (verse 7)? Envision yourself there – alone with God. What emotions are you feeling?

2. *Tav* (the end) is compared to a mountain climber, who reaches the peak and accomplishes their goal. Has there been a moment in your life when you experienced *tav*? Describe that moment. Or, are you still climbing? If you gave up the climb, what stood in your way?

3. Patty's adventure with God began with a plea to Him. That plea had four components: Surrender, Prayer, Faith/Fleece, and Trust. Have you ever heard the phrase, *once begun is half-way done?* Surrender is where change begins. Does the word *surrender* frighten you? If so, why?

4. When Patty's faith was tested, she fell back on fleece; asking God for a sign. She explains that using fleece instead of faith proved she needed to grow more in faith. Are you one to place a fleece before God, or do you stand in faith alone?

5. There are 9 treasures in the *Bag of Blue*. In Galatians 5:22-23, God identifies 9 qualities He treasures in us; they are 9 fruits of the Spirit. List them here. Is there one (or more) of the fruit that you find challenging? What single step can you take to improve in that area?

6. What did you learn about God or yourself through this chapter?

ABOUT THE AUTHOR

Patty Williams and family live in Upstate New York... her happy place. Two dogs, a cat, and a rather large pet pig (Charlie) round out their home; which is always bustling with activity. Patty and John enjoy their daily walks. Occasionally, they'll make a trip to the Adirondacks to climb a mountain. One of their goals is to bag all 46 High Peaks in the Adirondacks. So far, they've reached 13 summits. God willing and knees, ankles and backs cooperating – they'll achieve their goal.

Saint Patrick's Church, in Binghamton, is their home Parish. She and John are both involved in various ministries there. Patty facilitates Bible Study programs, small group gatherings, and an occasional day retreat. John lectors, and co-facilitates small group events with Patty.

When God leads Patty to write, she *usually* does what He's asked, but this book really tested her faith. She couldn't understand why He would ask her to write about roadside trash, but as they say —hindsight is 20/20. In writing this story, her relationship with Him grew. Her hope is that whoever reads *A Bag of Blue* will be drawn into a deeper relationship with God too.

NOTES

[1]   A Spoonful of Sugar. Words and music by Richard M. Sherman & Robert B. Sherman, 1963 for the 1964 Disney film, Mary Poppins.

Made in the USA
Columbia, SC
08 September 2024

42012090R20076